DATE DUE

INSIDE INTERNAL REVENUE

Inside
Internal Revenue

By WILLIAM SURFACE

COWARD-McCANN, INC. • NEW YORK

To Betsy

Acknowledgments

Several persons' cooperation was needed for *Inside Internal Revenue*. Thanks is due: My wife, Betsy, for her research and editing; Richard Schultz, for typing draft after draft of the same chapters; the Internal Revenue Service's public information officers who arranged interviews inside IRS's national, regional and district offices; taxpayers, accountants, former IRS employees, and U.S. senators and representatives and their staffs who yielded valuable insight but, either by request or the nature of editorial organization, often remain unidentified; and John Geoghegan and Ellis Amburn of Coward-McCann for their confidence in the proposed book.

Contents

1

The Season

He knew the story would infuriate the President. So George Reedy, then White House news secretary, laid the *Washington Star* on President Johnson's desk without, as he usually did, marking the article in question with a red crayon. The story's headline, however, did not escape Johnson's attention: NINETEEN HUNDRED AND SIXTY-FOUR TRAP CLOSES—LOANS BOOM IN TAX LAMENT. And the President needed only to read the first paragraph to grasp the theme:

Loan companies and banks are enjoying an unprecedented bonanza from cash-short taxpayers who failed to heed the warning that last year's tax cut had a built-in pitfall.

The President was piqued because similar negativism had circulated for a week. The Suburban Trust Company in Washington, D.C., for example, had disclosed that applications for loans to pay income taxes had risen almost 90 percent. Washington's Household Finance Corporation said that its business had increased 8 percent. Maryland's National Bank advertised: IF YOU NEED MONEY FOR TAXES DON'T BORROW FROM BILLY'S PIGGY BANK. In New York, an ad depicted a beggar approaching a matronly lady and asking: "Could You Spare A Dime Lady? I Have to Phone Bank of Commerce And Arrange A $5,000 Loan to Pay My Income Tax."

The Great Income Tax Cut of 1964 had, to use an old phrase, reached the moment of truth. Only 13 months before, in an election year, Johnson signed a bill that he said would reduce income taxes by $11.5 billion. For emphasis, the President singled out individuals who earned $5,200 a year and told a nationwide television audience, "Your take-home pay will go up around $10 a month." Larger take-home pay did result from the White House's direct order to the Senate Finance Committee: Lower the minimum amount of taxes that can be withheld from wages from 18 to 14 percent. No mimeographed press releases, however, explained that (1) the lowest rate of federal taxation in 1964 actually was 15.6 percent; and (2) that most of the revenue lost in reducing income tax rates would be, by mid-1966, retrieved by eliminating some tax deductions, increasing Social Security taxes, and adding or raising "user" taxes on items such as aviation and boat fuel.

But March 31, 1965, the day that Johnson laid aside the *Star*, was during the income tax paying season. And millions of Americans laboring through Internal Revenue Forms 1040 and 1040A had compared the lines stating "Amount of Tax Withheld" and "Total Amount Due" and were disturbed. Taxpayers who normally received a $25 refund owed about $75. Many individuals, of course, owed much more. By the next morning, Johnson had decided to soften the impact. One of his secretaries then went to the White House's West Wing, where about 40 reporters sat on dark green leather couches, and said, "Press, please go to the Cabinet Room." They walked to the room, chilled so that the President appears cool and relaxed under the harsh television cameras, to cover a ceremony for the Crusade Against Cancer postage stamp. There Johnson, standing beside his black leather chair, smiled and began: "This year I borrowed the money, the other day, to pay the government a tax of $100,000. They have a procedure where they pay it to the President with the left hand and take it out with the right."

It seemed remarkable that the President of the world's wealthiest nation and the richest President in United States history would announce that he had to borrow (from an unnamed bank in Texas) to pay his taxes. The announcement also might seem amusing to the few government employees who know that most of the President's taxes on his biweekly paycheck of $7,942 are paid in advance. But, when taxpayers heard on evening newscasts that President Johnson *also* had had to borrow to pay taxes, their dilemma did not seem so unique. Public criticism about the "phony tax cut" ended. Once again, in the Age of Taxation, Americans responded by being the world's most obedient taxpayers.

This type of theatricalism differs from tax season to tax season, but its effectiveness helps make the United States government's tax collectors—the Internal Revenue Service—a genuinely remarkable operation. Alternately friendly and frightening showmanship, plus broad authority, has shaped the Internal Revenue Service into the largest, most successful monetary collection organization of all time. The Service, as employees call IRS, needs to spend only 45 cents to collect every hundred dollars in taxes, less than one third the cost incurred by Canada's tax collectors and half that of Britain or France. As a result, the Service is more than the envy of most free world governments. Fifty-one nations have sent cabinet-level officials to Internal Revenue's National Office in Washington, D.C., to study how IRS persuades American corporations to pay "voluntarily" up to 48 percent of their profits in taxes and the average individual to work 2 hours and 19 minutes of each 8-hour day to pay taxes (including local taxes).

Yet the Internal Revenue Service, per se, remains faceless. Ask most Americans "who are our tax collectors?" and perhaps a few, if that, can name the Commissioner of Internal Revenue. This personal identity exists because the commissioner, as Internal Revenue's only political appointee (the most recent commissioner, crew-cut Sheldon S. Cohen, was at one time a tax lawyer for Lady Bird Johnson) makes most of Internal Revenue's announcements. Neither the commissioner nor the National Office has direct taxing power, but largely translates tax laws, written in generalities by the Treasury Department and Congressional committees, into specific regulations.

The actual tax collectors are the 63,516 Civil Service employees mostly situated in 58 district headquarters that are answerable to 1 of 7 regional offices. Virtually all of these employees remain anonymous outside the Service, except when a regional commissioner makes a speech. Not even the names of the special agents who trap the nation's most flagrant tax evaders are more than rarely mentioned in news accounts. Theoretically all Internal Revenue employees share a major case and this policy, of course, prevents anyone from becoming a personality. But, significantly, when the public sees or deals with any employee from IRS, it often pictures the person as a composite of what it hears about Internal Revenue. Or as a National Office's memorandum to district personnel said: "You're considered 'Mr. Revenue' by the public."

Internal Revenue has, to be sure, developed a powerful group personality that incongruously projects a dual image. In some respects, IRS is comparable to a beautiful woman who unpredictably kisses and kicks with equal passion. First, IRS wants to be known as a fair organization that collects taxes that are legally due, not one penny more. IRS not only desires a reputation for giving a service to taxpayers, but its name even embellishes this wish. Actually named the *Bureau* of Internal Revenue until 1953, it was retitled "Internal Revenue Service" to emphasize, as the Bureau's memo to the Treasury Department suggested, the "important service to taxpayer's side of revenue administration."

Since that time—particularly in 1961–62—directives from Internal Revenue's National Office urged regional officers to devote "strenuous efforts to gain widespread news coverage" and give "priority" to training a "corps of individuals who can most successfully convey a desirable image of the Service." Subsequently, the point that the "corps" has repeatedly stressed is that Internal Revenue has encouraged taxpayers to be so honest that an astonishingly high 96.7 percent of all tax receipts come from what is called "voluntary self-assessment."

5

The "voluntary assessment" is an argumentative point: seventy-five percent of individuals' taxes are withheld by employers, leaving little latitude not to pay, and corporations such as distilleries must pay taxes before whiskey is permitted to be poured into bottles. Too, there is the ominous threat of prison sentences for *non*-volunteers. This image has moved Senator Edward V. Long of Missouri to bluntly declare: "We hear much about the 'voluntariness' of our tax system, and there is much to be said for it. But frequently, the taxes which are 'voluntarily' paid are paid because of the roughest kind of threats and the apparent prospect of great cost and great retribution facing those who choose to disagree with IRS. Tax collection should be done with a minimum of fear, threats and intimidation and harassment."

IRS's other image is one of fear. So much apprehension emerges from Internal Revenue that the phrase "tax scare season" could be added to Benjamin Franklin's accurate prophecy: "But in this world nothing is certain but death and taxes." Invariably, as the April 15 deadline for filing federal tax returns approaches, Internal Revenue begins its psychological warfare by announcing "impact items" that are designed to strike a little terror into the hearts of anyone vacillating between honesty, evasion or taking a marginal deduction. The technique, as described by a former IRS special agent, involves keeping a large tax fraud case "on the back burner of the stove and just cooking slowly, then bringing it forward to the front burner right around the time that tax returns have to be filed." Throughout each February, March and April, the most conspicuous prosecutions for alleged tax evasion are released to illustrate that Internal Revenue just doesn't

6

miss any offenders. Most such examples of the horrible consequences of tax fraud—up to five years' imprisonment and a $10,000 fine for each offense—usually become prominent front-page items in many daily newspapers.

When individual cases fail to have national news potential, the nation is thoroughly covered by local cases. Consider what occurred on February 24, 1966: In Santa Ana, California, the federal government confiscated the city's only bus service because it owed past taxes, leaving many commuters searching for new transportation and mindful of Internal Revenue. In Chicago, a government complaint was filed (resulting in a grand jury indictment) against Dr. Stevan Durovic, who had been acquitted a month earlier of charges of defrauding the public with an asserted anticancer drug named Krebiozen, alleging that he had evaded $904,907.05 in taxes during 1960–62. In Brooklyn, a doctor, an insurance broker, a salesman, two lawyers and two brothers, occupations unannounced, were indicted for alleged tax evasion or failure to file returns. The pattern was repeated roughly every 10 days until April 15.

In previous years, individual cases have been more dramatic:

● On March 14, 1965, James (Jimmy Doyle) Plumeri, called a Mafia extortionist and "lamprey eel type of person who lives off other people's income," was sentenced to 2½ years in prison for omitting $7,000 on his income tax return.

● On April 8, 1964, Judge Earl Welch, 72, an Oklahoma State Supreme Court Justice since 1932, and Judge Nelson S. Corn, 80, another Oklahoman, were indicted (and later convicted) for evading $13,364 and $11,063 in taxes, respectively. The announcement contained high publicity possibilities since Judge Corn had recently announced: "No tax dodger should ever be elected to public office."

• On April 15, 1964, as seven million procrastinators still held their tax returns, William G. Stratton, former two-term governor of Illinois, was indicted on charges of failing to declare $93,595 (tax bill: $46,676) in campaign contributions that he had allegedly spent for personal use. Stratton was acquitted 11 months later.

• On April 28, 1963, as 700,000 Americans still had not filed their tax returns (and at least half had little intention of doing so until pressured), James M. Landis, former dean of the Harvard Law School and an advisor to two Presidents, was indicted (and later sentenced to 30 days in custody) for failing to file a return for five years.

• On February 27, 1962, an announcement was made that J. Truman Bidwell, chairman of the New York Stock Exchange's Board of Governors, had been indicted for allegedly evading $55,908 in taxes. Bidwell said the matter had been under discussion for three years and was released for publicity. He later was acquitted by a federal jury.

• During the 1962 tax filing period, Internal Revenue announced that 30 of its special agents had "invaded" Arkansas' Dallas County to check nearly 1,000 of the area's 10,522 citizens' tax returns and found a "bonanza" of persons who had not filed returns. More "invasions" appeared imminent.

The sequel to these cases is an announcement made each March that reminds short-memoried taxpayers about the previous year's criminal tax evaders. One lead: "Last year, approximately 1,400 convictions for tax evasion resulted in 293 years in prison, 2,269 years on probation, and $2.6 million in fines." Moreover, in writing such announcements, no cliché is left unturned if it fits the scare theme. Most press releases about catching tax evaders reveal that Internal Revenue has "redoubled its efforts," "instigated vigorous prosecution," has "begun acceleration," has "continued acceleration," "zeroed in on the foolish few" and devised "relentless methods" that will "bring to light the foolish few."*

Apart from this practice of publicizing tax evaders, two additional steps occurred during Mortimer Caplin's administration as Commissioner of Internal Revenue from February 7, 1961, to July 10, 1964. An extrovertish law professor with a penchant for historical images, bow ties and jokes about taxes ("Last year was the 50th anniversary of the income tax amendment to the Constitution, but the Internal Revenue Service somehow didn't seem to get any birthday cakes"), Caplin decided that if President John Kennedy could name his fresh administration the "New Frontier," he would lead Internal Revenue to what he called a "New Direction." As Caplin urged other IRS

---

* Such phrases and emphasis on catching tax evaders also are supposed to "comfort" taxpayers. States the Commissioner of Internal Revenue's 1965 Annual Report: "The results of the work of special agents is not measured solely by the number of criminal cases investigated or prosecutions recommended. Of paramount importance is the increase in voluntary compliance by the taxpaying public resulting from the impact of these investigations and subsequent successful prosecution of violators. Honest taxpayers, who comprise the vast majority, thus are reassured and potential tax fraud perpetrators receive a deterrent warning. Therefore, in a relentless effort to further the improvement of voluntary compliance, the tax fraud investigation program is directed toward the identification, investigation and prosecution of tax fraud cases in all sections of the country, in all strata of society, and involving all types of taxes."

9

officials: "We all should understand that the Service is not simply running a direct enforcement business aimed at making $2 billion in additional assessments . . . Our chief mission is to encourage and achieve more effective voluntary compliance." To promote this point, the Commissioner even wrote a letter to *Show*, then a magazine devoted to the arts, that outlined how his New Direction *artistically* collected taxes.

Caplin's subsequent tactics to cultivate "voluntary" compliance, however, were contradictory. He mentioned —and even a commissioner's intimations are analyzed and circulated by tax advisory services as possible new regulations—that major "crackdowns" were forthcoming. Internal Revenue, Caplin hinted, might allow a maximum of about $10 a day per person to be deducted from gross business income for travel and entertainment. Naturally, this hint alarmed businessmen, who knew that a modest hotel room in New York City costs $16 a day. Their excitement was heightened if they watched television in the hotel room during the 1963 tax scare season. Although the Federal Communication Commission recommends heavy fines and/or prosecution for showing misleading commercials on television, Internal Revenue aired a 20-second animated cartoon that depicted businessmen as cynical expense-account cheaters. The commercial, which opened with a scene of a bloated, night-clubbing businessman bouncing a blonde on his lap, had this dialogue:

Businessman: "Baby, this is living!"

Narrator: "Excuse me, sir, how can you afford all this?"

Businessman: "Expense-account living. Got my own company. Just write it off as a business expense. You can do it. What's your company?"

Narrator: "The Internal Revenue Service makes sure expense account deductions are for bona fide business-incurred expenses."

The cartoon ended with a brusque impression that Internal Revenue would "get" any businessman escorting a blonde. Not only did several Congressmen denounce the cartoon as "vicious," but it is said that the late President Kennedy was so irritated by the "public service message" that he called an assistant to get the "thing" off the air. Regardless of what occurred, Internal Revenue withdrew the cartoon the next day.

Nevertheless, the cartoon, and more of Caplin's speeches, implied that IRS might disallow any expenses if the business transpired at a restaurant that offered entertainment (not a "quiet business setting") and distracted from business conversations. The implication was so noticeable that the National Restaurant Association accused the Commissioner of starting an economic recession. Notably, E. M. Loew, owner of New York's Latin Quarter nightclub and head of a New England theater circuit, threatened to sue Caplin to correct what he termed inequities against expense accounts. "Either I have to go out of business or go to court," he told Caplin. Ultimately the Commissioner quietly retreated. The "crackdown," in essence, resulted in a new regulation that required taxpayers to substantiate all expenses with records, where practical, and to furnish receipts for business expenditures over $25—something already done by responsible individuals or businesses.

Simultaneously, Caplin's "human touch" approach produced a scare for everyone. Internal Revenue appeared to be converting itself into a computerized Big Brother.

Internal Revenue had, since 1948, been gradually install-
ing Automatic Data Processing, an intricate computer
system that is used by such diverse organizations as New
York's Consolidated Edison to compile monthly utility
bills and the Library of Congress to catalog books. In
1961, Internal Revenue dedicated the first of seven regional computer centers in Atlanta, Georgia, and a national computer center, which maintains a master list of
taxpayers, at Martinsburg, West Virginia. The computers
will vastly improve the system of processing tax returns.
But, as Caplin began speaking at luncheon clubs and
gatherings, an impression that Internal Revenue had more
than mere IBM computers began to spread. Taxpayers
either heard, or left Caplin's speeches maintaining, that
the Service had a "Martinsburg Monster" that had an
"infallible brain," "lurked," and "uncovered bonanzas."
Not only did Caplin sermonize much like Evangelist Billy
Graham, he used a similar "Hour of Decision" theme. As
Caplin warned New York's Board of Trade: "Now is the
time for taxpayers to climb on board" before "the computers will disclose by a push of the button who. . . ."

Indeed, converts to honest taxation came forth. And
they continued to repent for two years after Caplin left
the Internal Revenue Service. IRS personnel have told
news media that persons whom the Martinsburg Monster
has frightened into voluntarily confessing their tax sins,
some dating back to 1918, include: An 80-year-old grandmother, an 83-year-old New Jersey businessman, a middle-
aged Chicago undertaker, a young southern salesman, and
a New England pensioner. But these people did not
merely confess. They admittedly had been "weeping,"
"trembling," "scared," "fearing all hell would break loose,"

The Season

and "fortified with whiskey in order to face IRS." One man who had never filed a return even waited on an Internal Revenue agent's doorstep for daylight so he could confess and beg for leniency.

Cumulative publicity about the infallible ADP computers has not excited just a few neurotics. It has made a measurable impact upon thousands of taxpayers, maintains Clinton L. Walsh, a calm, courteous man who is IRS's Director of Operations for Automatic Data Processing. "From January, 1962, to July, 1965, at least a thousand person have voluntarily written or showed up at district offices and paid $5.2 million in delinquent taxes," Walsh explained, glancing at an interoffice memo. "This figure just includes persons who said—now we didn't ask them—that news about the computers had encouraged them to pay up before they were caught. There's no telling how many who've quietly paid were motivated by the computers. Why, the first year after the computers were installed in the Southeast Region, 45 percent more tax returns reported interest received from bank accounts and 20 percent more reported dividends from stocks. Besides, 7.7 percent more returns were filed in that region alone than had been received the previous year."*

Effective as publicizing "crackdowns" and infallible computers has been in moving tax cheaters to change their ways, many alarmed evaders are not delivering their money to Internal Revenue offices. Innumerable persons have stopped dealing in checks and started asking for untraceable currency. That cash apparently is being deposited into safety deposit boxes, not bank accounts, a

* The remainder of the nation, then not under the ADP system, showed only a 5 percent rise in the number of returns filed.

13

development supported by one fact. Banks have received such increased demands for $50, $100, $500 and $1000 bills that U.S. currency in circulation—which is money outside of Federal Reserve Banks—rose from $32.1 billion to $42 billion between 1961 and 1966. This change means that every man, woman and infant is carrying an average of $214 despite the record increase in the use of credit cards and checking accounts during the same five-year period. Internal Revenue officials concede that agents have found more and more large denomination currency in deceased persons' safety deposit boxes since the publicization of the computers, but maintains that it is only one factor in the currency shortage.

Not all of Internal Revenue's frightening propaganda, though, originates from IRS personnel. Anytime the Service's techniques are dramatized by Congressional investigators, the ensuing publicity magnifies many people's fear of the tax collectors. In 1965, for example, the Senate Subcommittee on Administrative Practice and Procedure revealed six instances where overzealous IRS agents secretly opened first-class mail and wiretapped telephones of suspected tax evaders. The investigation provoked the subcommittee chairman, Senator Edward Long of Missouri, to state: "Let there be no question about this. If we wish to avoid having a police state in America, we had better wake up and do something about it soon." Yet the most striking reaction to the incidents was to spread additional alarm. Several tax accountants and lawyers in cities such as New York and Pittsburgh said that they were afraid to use coin-operated public telephones in or near Internal Revenue's District Office buildings because the phones might be wiretapped. Whether or not IRS monitors conversations from public telephone booths is not the most relevant point. Some taxpayers believe that telephone conversations are intercepted.

Starkly put, the fact is that already Internal Revenue's use of the scare, innuendo, and threat of severe or embarrassing punishment has created an *imaginary* secret police in the United States today. Make no mistake. This "secret police" is purely visionary. But the fear of such a police exists, causing some individuals to harbor thoughts that a Big Brother can "get" them for something that may or may not be on their tax return.

Just how the tax collectors can deliberately punish even the toughest villain alive is demonstrated each time that the federal government publicizes a crusade to convict master criminals. Look at the list of America's most notorious—and hence most investigated—racketeers, con men, murderers and corrupt political bosses from 1930 to 1966: Al Capone, the Prohibition era's No. 1 racketeer; his gunman, Frank (The Enforcer) Nitti; Paul (The Waiter) Ricca, Capone's eventual successor in the 1950's as Chicago's alleged crime syndicate leader; Frank Costello, often called chairman of the board of New York's infamous Murder, Inc.; Albert Anastasia, reputed triggerman for Murder, Inc.; Mickey Cohen, allegedly the West Coast's No. 1 racketeer; and Thomas (Boss) Pendergast, Kansas City's late political despot. All the federal and local government's investigative resources could not produce evidence to convict *any* of these men of their apparent crimes. But Internal Revenue proved that each mobster spent considerably more money than he reported as taxable income and sent *every one* to prison for evading taxes.

As has been recognized since Biblical times, the power to tax is the power to oppress. Today that power is feared by two broad categories of taxpayers: (1) the knowledgeable individuals who understand precisely how the Internal Revenue Service could harass them, and (2) individuals with minimal knowledge of Internal Revenue's practices who simply imagine how IRS might punish them. Take, as an example of the first category, major corporations. Most corporate executives realize that Internal Revenue's politically appointed commissioner could, if told, interpret an elastic law that could financially injure them: for instance, simply rule whether the profits received from the sale of stocks, real estate or other assets was a long-term capital gains transaction in which the maximum tax is 25 percent, or should be taxed at a corporation's regular rate of up to 48 percent. Though the corporation has an even chance in court of reversing an unfavorable ruling, the defense can be costly and the company's stock values can drop during the process.

Such a threat—or the equally effective *rumor* of a threat—was illustrated in November, 1965 when the aluminum industry raised prices by two percent. Since industry price increases can initiate an inflationary chain reaction, they often bring quick interventions from the government. In the Administration's so-called shadow war against the aluminum corporations, industry executives clearly said that they were being "clubbed," "pressured," and "given ultimatums where it hurts." Subsequent tactics, such as the government's releasing aluminum from its National Strategic Stockpile to suppress aluminum prices, exemplified that leverage could be used. Still, as Leon E. Hickman, executive vice president of Aluminum Company of America (Alcoa), announced, Alcoa had "no present intention of canceling" the price increase. Then the *Wall Street Journal,* whose executives maintain close contact with industry, reported that a White House "emissary" had specifically threatened Hickman or John D. Harper, Alcoa's president, with a full-scale tax review.

Naturally such charges, whether fact or fiction, must be answered. The White House's denial called the story "absolutely false, just plain hogwash." But, in a standard government practice in cases where denials might be discredited later, the refutation came from Joseph Califano, then a little-known special assistant who normally would not know if such a threat had occurred. Thus, if the denial was proven wrong later, another White House spokesman need only say: "The spokesman was not fully aware of all the facts." Alcoa, meanwhile, said nothing more, leaving the impression that the threat of a tax investigation was, indeed, true. Significantly, the aluminum industry *did* rescind its price increase.

Similar possibilities of Administration-ordered intimidation by the Internal Revenue Service worry Congressmen who criticize government programs. A few of these admit that they pay a "little extra tax" to avoid any charge that they spent surplus tax-exempt contributions to political campaigns for personal benefits and thereby consciously evaded taxes on unreported income. One senator, John J. Williams of Delaware, received a briefing on Internal Revenue's authority in 1964. Why? First, Williams is an investigative senator who has exposed irregularities within Internal Revenue since 1951. Secondly, he was the man who laid a legal-size manila folder on Senate Majority Leader Mike Mansfield's desk in October, 1963, and said, "And I don't have it all yet." Still, there was enough in the file to indicate how Robert Baker, the Senate's majority secretary, had found employment so inspiring under the Capitol Dome that in only eight years he parlayed a salary that ranged from $8,000 to $19,600 into a purported $2 million empire. Would Baker answer Williams' questions about possible conflict of interest? No. Instead Baker quit. And Williams introduced a Senate resolution that demanded formal investigation of Baker and, in effect, began the headlined "Bobby Baker Mess." Twice when Williams felt the investigation was a "whitewash," he introduced new evidence that first became a Presidential campaign issue, then forced the embarrassed Senate to reopen the inquiry.

A steady campaign of planted smears and watching his mail did not stop Williams. Then a letter from Internal Revenue ordering Williams to prepare to "substantiate" information on a two-year-old income tax return compelled him to interrupt the investigation. Such an audit, Williams realized, would require that he study his receipts and canceled checks to document each line of his return. He did just that, and when his fatiguing three-hour interrogation with an Internal Revenue auditor ended, the auditor said that Williams owed $30.16 in additional taxes, plus $1.74 for interest. Although Williams and his accountant both felt the assessment was erroneous, the senator wrote out a check. "I just want to get this nit-picking over with," Williams said. "This thing's just a nuisance, that's all there is to it." Williams' interpretation that he did not owe additional taxes was proven two months later. He received a form letter from the Internal Revenue Service stating that the Service had made an error and owed *him* $30.16. Enclosed was a check refunding the $30.16, plus the Senator's earlier payment of $31.90.

Asked about Williams' charges that the timing and tediousness of the audit indicated that he was being harassed, an officer at IRS's Mid-Atlantic Regional office answered: "A young auditor went to Washington and audited Senator Williams' return, then just made a mistake. He put a figure on the wrong line and it looked like the Senator owed the extra tax. There was no harassment and the District Director knew nothing about it." Again, the point is that, whether Williams was or was not deliberately given a nuisance audit, he felt intimidated.

Now consider the feelings of taxpayers whom statisticians call the "millions of average Americans." Evidently millions of them fear Internal Revenue much as the reporter-copy editor employed by the Chicago *Tribune* who reverently calls himself a "sportswriter." Yet he always lists his occupation as what he calls a less glamorous "copyreader" on his income tax form so that he admittedly "won't attract attention." He does this even though his return includes no itemized deductions and nothing that interests Internal Revenue's auditors or investigators. How can it be surmised that millions hold similar apprehensions? A giant tax-preparation business thrives, partly to fill out taxpayers' 1040 and 1040A income tax forms and partly to reassure them that, as one often hears, "We'll keep you out of trouble with the tax people."

The H.&R. Block Tax, Inc., Kansas City, Missouri, for instance, which has over a thousand offices in 49 states servicing what it calls the "working man's return," flourishes largely because it avoids "the fear aspects of our

19

complex tax system." Block, too, stresses this point in the mimeographed press releases that it sends to branch offices with suggestions that the manager add his name to the blank spaces in the material. One such release about Block's services emphasizes: " 'We sell peace of mind,' is the way Mr. _____ words it."

Block's firms do complete taxpayers' returns and advertise that they guarantee accuracy. Smaller businesses, however, apparently subsist entirely on people's reservations about tax collectors. One such group, which calls itself the "American Cooperating Taxpayers (ACT)" of Rochester, New York, placed a small ad in the *New York Times Magazine* that began: "UNJUSTLY TREATED BY INTERNAL REVENUE? A cooperating association of American taxpayers has been formed for the purpose of providing legal and accounting assistance to members who feel they have been unfairly treated by the Internal Revenue Service." A letter to ACT, requesting any further information about how it counters or can document any abuse, brought only a leaflet and application card. The card read: "Enroll me as a member . . . I enclose the membership fee of $25.00 and $3.00 for the first quarterly assessment to the protection fund ($28.00 in all). I agree to pay the other three quarterly assessments as they are billed to me."

Evidently, Internal Revenue's current administrators sensed that the Service's scare approach was sufficient and, therefore, it needed no *new* psychological tactics. That was indicated when, after Sheldon Cohen was appointed Commissioner of Internal Revenue in 1965, he said that he would not emulate Mortimer Caplin's campaign-style speeches and would attempt to improve Internal Revenue's public image. Subsequently, Internal Revenue spent $20,000 in taxpayers' money to employ Lippincott & Margulies, Inc., a management design firm on New York's Park Avenue, to create that improved image. What did taxpayers receive for the money? The firm decided that Internal Revenue's seal—a dotted shield with scales, key and olive branch*—was too cluttered. The upshot: Internal Revenue's 1966 tax forms displayed a new symbol that was dominated by a drawing of a ferocious eagle. Unlike any other eagle used on government documents, this one appeared explicitly mean and symbolized iron-fisted authority. (This change moved Tax Foundation, Inc., to comment: "The eagle may be redesigned, but the forms remain an art designed to pluck the most feathers with the least squawks.")

The eagle, of course, wasn't meant to soften Internal Revenue's image because scare and secrecy are two of IRS's most effective techniques of fostering semivoluntary compliance. A human element exists who would not pay their taxes if they didn't dread IRS. But do Internal Revenue's operations befit its public image? Before examining how Internal Revenue does collect taxes, it seems imperative to ask: How and why did the United States develop this monolithic system of tax gatherers in the first place?

* The scales symbolize equal treatment and justice, the olive branch represents fairness and courtesy.

2

Birth of the Bite

Ironically the Internal Revenue Service functions in a
nation settled by tax-haters. Just as quickly as America's
Thirteen Colonies assessed light tariffs and poll or property taxes to pay salaries of governors, judges and other
officials, ingenious tactics often emerged to minimize
them. Notably, Rhode Island's residents decided that the
only democratic process would be to vote on the taxable
value of their neighbor's property. The system produced
such mutually low estimates and easy concealment of
assets that it eventually was terminated.

A centralized government's attempts to tax the Colonies
was even less successful. Colonial Britain's decision to
impose an internal tax, partially necessitated by its costly
defenses in Spanish Florida and French Canada, met with
violent reaction from tavern-keepers, merchants, printers
and lawyers. When Britain's Parliament passed the Stamp
Act of 1765—which taxed every newspaper, pamphlet,
advertisement, doctor's license and playing card in the

Colonies—a well-organized mob forced a British officer at New York's Battery to burn the stamps publicly. Such dissension and a boycott of English imports compelled Parliament to repeal the tax. Stunned, Britain's finance minister, Charles Townshend, gave the House of Commons an emotional one-hour speech on taxation, which was interrupted by opponents' jeers that he was afraid to tax Americans. He left exclaiming: "I will! I will!"

The subsequent Townshend Act of 1767, levying taxes on certain English manufactured goods and tea entering the Colonies, was also brief. Antitax groups organized by Samuel Adams, an unsuccessful businessman but successful propagandist, assembled to enjoy free rum and the shade of what they named the Liberty Tree near Boston's Common; then they printed handbills or wrote letters to the Boston *Gazette* describing exaggerated (and sometimes fictitious) scenes of the tax collectors' drunken abuse. Consequently, impassioned colonists again boycotted Britain's merchandise and harassed its garrisons, occasionally chanting "no taxation without representation," until the tax was removed from all imports except tea. But not before one radical group was so incited that it stoned British sentries until fired upon. Five agitators were killed and five tax martyrs born.

The incident, later depicted in a published drawing by Paul Revere as Redcoats shooting straight at innocent citizens, further stirred anti-British passions. To prolong this feeling, Adams' "Sons of Liberty" continued guerrilla-style tactics against King George's so-called "hateful tea tax." Ultimately, extremists disguised as Mohawk Indians and Negroes sneaked aboard three of the East India Company's ships and pushed 342 crates of tea into Boston's harbor. The destruction brought forth Britain's reprisals and provided the colonists' initial impetus to separate from England.

This mistrust of centralized taxation was not limited to Britain. When Colonial representatives met to unite against England's authority, they even withheld the power to tax from their own Continental Congress. The necessity for taxes, however, became evident during attempts to finance the Revolutionary War of 1775–83. Yet the colonists apparently considered any means of collecting revenue more honorable than by federal taxation—the Continental Congress authorized a lottery to raise expenses. Such prominent men as George Washington, John Hancock and Benjamin Franklin helped promote the sale of 100,000 tickets which, purchasers were told, would bring prizes ranging from $20 to $50,000. However, the first drawing, held in Philadelphia's College Hall, was distinguished more by complicated schemes than jubilant winners. After deducting 15 percent of the $500,000 receipts for expenses, the lottery managers subdivided the drawing into what was called "four classes." In the first drawing, all "winners" above $50 received bonds said to be redeemable in five years. The second drawing was postponed. The outcome of the other drawings is not clear.

Lotteries, though, were not enough. The Continentals also borrowed money from France, Holland and Spain. But the main revenue source resulted when the government introduced and printed paper currency, bonds and quartermaster notes that were to be redeemed from taxes levied and collected by the 13 states. Since the states also had to recruit militia to fight the tax-collecting enemy, they found enforcing such taxation impractical. Instead, the states collected flour, corn and rum and advancing armies often requisitioned merchandise, sometimes leaving the quartermaster notes or near-worthless paper money.

The rueful exercise in raising revenues taught the Revolutionary leaders to incorporate in the resultant Constitution of the United States of America, Article 1, Section 8: "The Congress shall have Power To lay and collect Taxes, Duties, Imposts and Excises, To pay the Debts and provide for the common Defence and general Welfare of the United States. . . ." This authority was soon used. In 1791, Alexander Hamilton, the first Secretary of the Treasury and an advocate of strong government, employed revenue collectors to gather excise taxes on whiskey, refined sugar, snuff, carriages, and sales of slaves, bonds, land and homes. Public indignation nearly matched that directed against the tea tax. Even a splinter political party gained recognition as the "Republicans" by campaigning against the Federalists' "hateful" tax. Another indication of the sentiment was shown in the House of Representatives, where Georgia's James Jackson prophetically roared: "The time will come when a shirt shall not be washed without an excise."

Moreover, rumors circulated that the government would charge $1 tax on every baby boy born, $10 on each baby girl and undetermined amounts on every wedding held and plow or hymn book sold. Since Bibles (plus an occasional hymn book or almanac) often were the only books available in frontier areas, they also were used to substantiate the evils of taxation. Joseph and Mary were in congested Bethlehem, many preachers sermonized, to pay old King Herod's census tax when Jesus was born in a manger. Congregations also read passages of the New Testament that reflected Jesus Christ's apparent low regard for tax collectors; "Look at him! A glutton and a drinker, a friend of tax-gatherers and sinners! . . . Many bad characters—tax-gatherers and others—were seated with him. . . . The lawyer of Pharisees said, 'He eats with tax-gatherers and sinners.' Jesus overheard and said to them, 'It is not the healthy that need a doctor, but the sick. I did not come to invite virtuous people, but sinners.' "

Another Biblical passage accepted literally was: "Let him drink and forget his poverty and remember his misery no more." The drink was bourbon whiskey, said to have been first distilled from barley, corn and rye by Reverend Elijah Craig, a weekend preacher. Since the government's tax on whiskey was 7 cents a gallon (the price was 25 cents a gallon), grass-roots protests erupted among the predominantly Irish and Scotch settlers in Western Pennsylvania, Maryland, Virginia, North Carolina, Virginia and central Kentucky, where one-sixth of the population's principal occupation was distilling whiskey. Since these settlers seldom drank tea, the whiskey tax seemed more inequitable than King George III's tea tax. Thus as an excise tax collector named Robert Johnson rode into Pigeon Creek, Pennsylvania, he became the first known agent to be pulled from his horse by distillers dressed in women's dresses and bonnets. Johnson's head was shaved, then he was tarred and feathered. When Johnson's supervisor rode out to serve a warrant on the tax avoiders, he also was tarred, feathered and left bound to a tree.

Similar terrorism continued against tax collectors until

it reached an ugly climax. Fanned by four rabble-rousers and the explosive combination of tax agents fatally shooting one distiller and serving warrants on about 50 others, nearly 5,000 armed, antitax rebels (also called "whiskey lovin' White Indians") formed a "scrub Congress" and marched into Pittsburgh for what they called a "visit" and the government termed The Whiskey Tax Rebellion of 1794. When Pennsylvania's governor refused to use the state militia, President Washington mobilized 13,000 troops, a force comparable to the Revolutionary War strength, to occupy Pittsburgh and arrest the few leaders who hadn't retreated to Kentucky. The agitation in Kentucky, though less violent, was more systematic. Tax agents' saddles were destroyed and the ears of their horses were clipped. And each morning men such as Colonel Thomas Marshall, Lexington's chief tax collector, found a pile of cow manure carefully planted by his door for him to step in.

It was not difficult to read the nation's mood. Thomas Jefferson was elected President in 1800 largely on a campaign to end what he called the "infernal excise system" that was "hostile to the genius of a free people." Excise taxes were quickly repealed. But the outbreak of the War of 1812 with England dramatized the need for more government revenue. Even Secretary of the Treasury Albert Gallatin, who had helped organize the Whiskey Tax Rebellion, ironically suggested an excise tax on common purchases, including whiskey. A later Secretary, Alexander J. Dallas, proposed, of all things, a tax on the incomes of lawyers, solicitors and public officials! The idea was dismissed by Congress' Ways and Means Committee on grounds that the tax would indicate such officials were overpaid. Eventually excise taxes were adopted, but again were repealed in 1817. For the next 43 years customs taxes on imports, plus sales of public lands, financed the government.

Suddenly the Civil War's enormous cost brought Americans their first tax on income and the birth of Internal Revenue. Congress' bill establishing a Commissioner of Internal Revenue was signed into law by President Abraham Lincoln on July 1, 1862, the same day that he signed a bill making polygamy a crime and for which he received equal space in the Washington *Star:* "The President has approved and signed the following important bills: The bill to provide internal revenue to defray the expenses of the Government and pay interest on the public debt."* The *Star's* same edition also noted that New York newspapers reported the New York Stock Exchange's sales had taken a "strong downward surge."

The tax rate, affecting only 1 percent of the population, was 3 percent on net incomes from $600 to $10,000 and 5 percent thereafter. Severe penalties for tax avoidance existed: Failure to file a tax return—if the tax avoider was caught—brought a $500 fine or a tax rate of 50 percent on all income with no right of appeal. Anyone who didn't pay his delinquent tax within 10 days after his name appeared in an advertisement or poster would have his property confiscated.

The income tax blank contained only 18 lines, but, like Internal Revenue Form 1040 issued a hundred years later, confused some of the best minds. Even Lincoln apparently misunderstood the tax: When his estate was settled 10 years after his death, his heirs received $1,279.15 that

* The Confederacy also enacted its own system of taxation on incomes.

he had overpaid in taxes. Moreover, the new tax's complexity wasn't simplified by Internal Revenue's early commissioners. The first, George S. Boutwell, a bearded lawyer and former governor from Massachusetts, was considered an able administrator. Starting with only one assistant in a ground-floor room at the Treasury Building, he built within six months a bureau of 3,882 men headed by 185 District Collectors, each given a certificate of confirmation signed by Lincoln. However, before Boutwell had completely organized Internal Revenue, he quit to campaign for (and win) a seat in Congress.

His successor, Joseph J. Lewis, was another bearded lawyer (from Pennsylvania) and, considering that he first suggested Lincoln as a presidential candidate, also, was a political appointee. Lewis made several improvements such as a directive to audit returns: "Let assistant assessors understand that it is their business not merely to take returns, but to ascertain whether they are correct. . . ." However, according to Boutwell, Lewis also personally answered many letters about tax questions and made rulings that contradicted those issued by Internal Revenue's section chiefs. Subordinates, who usually had to read Lewis' surprising decisions in newspapers, complained that morale was low. It was further deflated by another of the commissioner's decisions: he hired private tax collectors, a breed comparable to bounty hunters, at fees ranging up to 50 percent of any delinquent revenue they collected. Internal Revenue's full-time assistant assessors, paid from $3 to $5 a day, learned of the lucrative business when they frequently were ordered to accompany private collectors, who not always returned after collecting the taxes.

Another problem was taxpayers' shifting attitudes. Initially, since the Civil War also brought prosperity, most taxes were paid with minimal resentment and sometimes ostentatious patriotism. Characteristically, after author Mark Twain paid his 1864 tax of $36.82, including a delinquency penalty of $3.12, he wrote to the Virginia City (Nevada) *Territorial Enterprise:* "I am taxed on my income! This is perfectly gorgeous. I never felt so important in my life." By 1865, however, Twain, like thousands of others, objected to the doubling of the tax rate. When confronted by an Internal Revenue collector seeking unpaid taxes, Twain replied that he was "unaware that a Bureau of Internal Revenue existed." Even Lincoln had apologized for what he termed "inequities in the practical application of taxes." Accordingly, Congress appointed a U.S. Revenue Commission which found that Internal Revenue's administration was "very far from what it should be . . . and interfered with the private interests of wealthy and influential individuals." Furthermore, Congress in 1868 found that an income tax during peacetime was unnecessary, returned all surplus receipts to the states and, in 1872, repealed the income tax.

Again the government was financed by tariffs, plus excise taxes on items such as liquor* and oleomargarine, a new product, until an expansionist era began in 1893. As the government began to spend heavily for projects such as an expanding Navy, tariffs were increased. Prices on

---

* Hatred for the whiskey tax had not entirely subsided. After 83 of Internal Revenue's whiskey tax collectors were killed or wounded by snipers over one four-year period, the government dispatched General George Armstrong Custer's cavalry into the whiskey belt. Custer made such an impressive show of strength that he then was promoted to subduing rebellious Indians in a career that led to the ill-fated battle at Little Big Horn.

some imports became prohibitive. Frequent bank and
business failures also occurred and the cost of living was
to rise 25 percent over the next 10 years. Possible tariff
reforms were heatedly debated. Then a coalition of western and southern congressmen, whose agrarian constitu-
ency had little cash income, helped push through an
amendment to the Wilson-Gorman Tariff Act of 1894 that
levied a 2 percent tax on incomes over $4,000. Quickly,
the Bureau of Internal Revenue reorganized its dormant
Income Tax Division. But it did so over vehement protests. The tax, warned Senator John Sherman of Ohio,
"was socialism, communism and devilism." Regardless of
how such an income tax might be described, the con-
servative Supreme Court ruled the next year that it was
unconstitutional on grounds that a direct federal tax was
forbidden unless it was apportioned among the states
according to population.

Once more, Internal Revenue's income tax division
closed even before it could collect the tax. But the federal
government's expenses needed it kept opened. The U.S.
had used its Navy to emerge from isolation and occupy
Hawaii, drive Spain from Cuba, then take or purchase
Puerto Rico, Guam, the Philippine Islands, and plan the
Panama Canal. Would these expenditures be financed by
an income tax like that already being collected in all
European nations and Australia, India and Japan? Again
Congressmen from the South and West wanted this
method of taxation because eastern financiers and manufacturers, not their populace, would largely pay it. Similar
but noisier pressures came from the Populist (Socialist),
Anti-Monopoly and Greenback Parties, who openly re-
sented ultrawealthy men such as J. Pierpont Morgan and

31

John D. Rockefeller. These parties were short-lived, but their crusades had some effect. In 1909, Congress ordered Internal Revenue to collect a 1 percent *excise* tax on corporations' profits above $5,000 a year as a privilege of doing business. The levy was a thin disguise for an unconstitutional income tax.

Meanwhile, President William Howard Taft's quiet meetings with congressional leaders at Maryland's Chevy Chase Country Club resulted in Congress proposing a 16th amendment to the Constitution, empowering the government to tax incomes "without apportionment among the several States and without regard to any census or enumeration." The amendment's chief sponsors were the Republicans, who opposed the income tax but felt certain that the states would refuse to ratify it and permanently kill the proposal. Surprisingly, by February, 1913, 42 of 48 states had ratified the amendment and revived the modern income tax.

The tax rate set by Congress was 1 percent on personal income from $3,000 to $20,000 with progressive rates up to 6 percent thereafter. It had little opposition among the general public simply because it was aimed at the rich. Typical sentiment was shown by the lead of a news story in the Washington *Evening Star:* "It's no joke. Some time during the fiscal year the happy possessors of so much income [$3,000] will have to pay a pro rate tax to support the government." Only one of every 271 Americans did possess enough money to pay the tax, a criterion that made taxpaying a status symbol. The affluent soon were drafted to pay even higher taxes. When the United States was pulled into Europe's murderous trench war with Germany in 1917, emergency tax rates were revised to range from 6 percent at the bottom to a maximum of 77 percent. By 1920, the Bureau of Internal Revenue had grown to 15,000 employees and collected what was called an "astonishing" $5.5 billion a year.

After the war, Congress passed five genuine tax reductions, revising the rate of taxation at 1½ to 25 percent despite the loss of taxes on whiskey following the Prohibition Act. However, the postwar recession deteriorated into the catastrophic Depression that left 13 million Americans unemployed, reduced tax collections to $1.5 billion and put Franklin D. Roosevelt in the White House in 1933 on the promise of a New Deal. Roosevelt's taxation philosophy ("social unrest . . . can only be prevented by very high taxes . . . Everybody should have the same income . . . nobody should have more than $25,000 a year") and the New Deal's programs of managed economy, public works, and welfare care that extended from premature babies to old-age pensions, bore a price that revolutionized taxation. Annual income tax collections quadrupled from $1.4 billion, or an average of $12.80 per person in 1933, to $7.4 billion, or $55.25 per person in 1941, when the preparation for possible wars against Germany and Japan stimulated the economy and replaced the New Deal's need for public works.

World War II brought even more dramatic increases: An emergency "Victory Tax" of 5 percent on all personal incomes above $624; a revision of regular income tax rates ranging from 19 to 88 percent of earnings; increased gift, estate and corporations' excess profits tax, up to a maximum of 80 percent; and new or higher excise taxes on tobacco, liquor, jewelry, furs, telephone calls, travel and gasoline. The tax on gas, for example, was 50 percent.

Roosevelt demanded higher taxes, but Congress instead adopted a suggestion from the Treasury Department and championed by Beardsley Ruml, chairman of the Federal Reserve Bank of New York: a pay-as-you-go tax program that produces revenue a year earlier and reduces the large number of delinquent bills the following year.

Called The Withholding Tax Act of 1943, the new law required employers to deduct tax liabilities from weekly paychecks.* Moreover, withholding was the least painful system for both Internal Revenue and the smaller salaried worker, who now paid income taxes for the first time. For one thing, it ended a common alibi given to Internal Revenue collectors: "I don't have the money." For another, as wartime earnings rose, most industrial workers' net "take-home pay" was larger than previously nontaxed earnings.

Nevertheless, as war debts increased, Roosevelt asked for much higher taxes on those he called "the economic Royalists." But Congress, recognizing that inheritance and corporation taxes already reached a staggering 80 percent, passed a bill that would: double excise taxes on luxury items, add only 1 percent to the income tax rate and freeze the tax rate for Social Security. Irate, Roosevelt vetoed the bill—the first tax bill ever vetoed by a President—as "wholly ineffective and providing relief not for the needy but for the greedy." Equally furious, Congress overrode the veto and passed the Individual Income Tax Act of 1944 that replaced the 5 percent Victory Tax with a 3 percent tax, adjusted income tax rates at 20 to 91

* Internal Revenue also was permitted to make partial forgiveness of unpaid tax bills for 1942 so that some persons would not be unduly burdened.

34

percent, allowed individual taxpayers to deduct from gross income $500 for themselves and each dependent, plus a standard 10 percent for personal expenses.

By 1945, Internal Revenue annually collected $43.6 billion in taxes, or an average of $312.13 for every man, woman and child in the United States. After World War II, Congress twice reduced the tax rate (the latter over President Truman's veto) and prepared to lower excise rates. But the United States' involvement in the Korean War and the age of foreign aid instead forced restoration of the previous tax cuts, revised income tax rates at 22 to 92 percent on incomes above $600. By 1953, when Korea's war ended, taxes totaled $69.7 billion, or a per-capita tax of $436.53 per year.

The dramatic reduction in taxes that had always followed cessation of war never came. Instead, federal spending—the only reason that taxes must be collected—tripled from 1950 to 1966. Two inescapable facts account for this. First, taking about half our tax dollar is the Cold War that requires global defenses against Communism and an accelerated missile program. Moreover, since Roosevelt introduced massive federal spending, each subsequent president must originate domestic assistance programs without curtailing previous commitments, or face harsh assessment. When, for example, President Dwight Eisenhower worked more to balance the federal budget than promote new administration programs, he soon was labeled by columnists as the President who "sat by the bedside." Polls by instant historians already rank Eisenhower near the bottom of the "average," or least-effective, category of Presidents. In contrast, an appraisal of "great" exists for Roosevelt and his New Deal; of "near great" for

Truman, who added his Fair Deal; and "inspiring" for John F. Kennedy, who began the New Frontier. Too, comparable evaluation seems assured for Lyndon Johnson, who said "let us continue" Kennedy's programs, then sponsored his expensive Great Society in an effort to build his own legend.

Yet the emergence of new presidential programs doesn't assure ceilings on older ones.* Consider the nation's population shift. The demise of an average of 356 farms each day during the 1960s has caused radical migration from rural areas to congested industrial cities and resulted in the creation in 1965 of a Department of Housing and Urban Development that spent $2.3 billion in its first full year and undertook plans to build a palacelike headquarters. Since farm population dwindled 20 percent, from 15,635,000 to 12,500,000, between 1960 and 1965, the U.S. Department of Agriculture's responsibilities should have decreased. Were the Agriculture Department's surplus employees transferred elsewhere? No. During the same period, the Department's number of employees *increased* 20 percent, from 98,694 to 117,481, and its annual expenditures rose from $4.9 billion to $7.9 billion.

Thus, big government has become the nation's biggest growth industry. In 1966, the federal government employed 2.7 million civilians, had 3 million persons on military payrolls, and paid at least 250,000 employees over $10,000 a year, a rate considerably higher than in any private industry. Furthermore, the government provides even better job security and fringe benefits, near-automatic raises and promotions, and 13 days a year in

* The *Encyclopedia of U.S. Government Benefits* alone totals 1,011 pages.

sick leave that can be accumulated for quicker retirement or, as a spot check made in Brooklyn and in Washington, D.C., in 1965 showed, were used by 282 persons to moonlight as cabdrivers.

In order to pay the $44.7 billion a year just to run the government's domestic operations, Internal Revenue Service must deposit more and more money into the Treasury Department's bank account. Therefore in 1965, Internal Revenue received $119.7 billion of the nation's $694.8 billion Gross National Product (the total amount spent for all goods and services). Internal Revenue collected $74.2 billion, or 62 percent from individual and corporation incomes; $14.6 billion from excise taxes on liquor, cigarettes, gasoline, telephone calls and plane tickets; $14 billion from taxes on inheritances and gifts, unemployment insurance receipts, and "fees" on items such as passports. The remaining $16.8 billion was collected for Social Security. Yet, all collections totaled $2.7 billion less than what the government spent during the year.

Thus a burden to raise more money exists.* The command passes from the White House, across Executive Avenue to the Treasury Department building's third floor, then three blocks down Pennsylvania Avenue to the Internal Revenue Service's National Office, a gray marble-columned building designed (in 1930) after once-hated Britain's waterfront Inland Revenue Building. The National Office, decentralized following exposure of nation-

---

* In the meantime, the government borrows the balance with a technique only slightly more sophisticated than ordering the U.S. Bureau of Printing and Engraving to print an extra $2.7 billion. The Treasury asks commercial banks to buy bonds totaling $2.7 billion and credit the money to the government's account. Then the Federal Reserve System pays the amount in question to the banks with "new money" and takes the government bonds.

wide internal scandals in 1951–52, no longer directly collects taxes. Headed by a commissioner, a deputy, six assistant commissioners and 23 division directors (plus a staff of 3,200), the National Office functions largely as a coordinator. It supervises all national publicity, planning, research and training programs; interprets rulings; and sees that policies, old and new, are uniform on all collection levels.

The trend in policy, as the need for revenue increases, is to subject larger portions of incomes to taxation through stricter computerized enforcement and legislation. New laws have required Internal Revenue, among other numerous changes, to either eliminate or reduce the number of previously deductible items such as sales taxes, liquor and cigarette taxes, tax-exempt sick pay, credit on stock dividends, and special preferences for some Americans living outside the United States.

The shift means that more and more money will be extracted from the tax returns processed by the 63,516 employees spread among Internal Revenue's 950 small local offices, 58 district offices (at least one is located in every state), and seven sprawling regional service centers —all supervised by one of seven regional offices. These offices are now annually deluged with 102.5 million tax returns, 340 million other IRS forms, and 150 million interoffice documents—enough paper to move a House of Representatives subcommittee to make an investigation and then write a report entitled "The Federal Paperwork Jungle." Each of these sheets of paper represents part of an American's life. And what Internal Revenue's employees decide to do, or not to do, with a tax return can affect almost any working adult.

3

Into the Paper Jungle

The influx of tax returns invariably begins each January 2 when persons needing money file early to get their refund checks for $18, $35 and sometimes $60. Some also attach letters expressing their urgency. "Please rush my refund," one letter asked. "You can take a 2 percent discount if you get it back to me in 10 days." Another handwritten note read: "Can I get a loan on this refund if you cannot rush? . . . If *I* can do *you* a favor, please don't hesitate to call on me."

From then on, the volume of incoming returns steadily increases until late February, then drops to an even flow through most of March. It is an expected lull, one that Internal Revenue's employees call "the lull before the storm." Suddenly 40 million returns—including many filed by large corporations employing full-time tax accountants—arrive like a paper avalanche at Internal Revnue's district offices during the two weeks before the April 15 deadline. Seventeen million returns, mostly from individuals and businesses who owe additional taxes, arrive from April 15 to 22. Then the current of returns eases back to a trickle, hundreds of thousands instead of millions, until early June.

The scene at all district offices is one of six-foot-high stacks of envelopes, and temporary employees apologetically bumping into regular employees, until activity becomes a maelstrom. Undoubtedly the most active scene is at New York's Manhattan District. Here during the peak filing period about a million tax returns from the nation's richest area pour into the new, 21-story granite and aluminum building that sits like an oasis on a grim block adjacent to the Keystone Bolt and Nut Company and the Tropical Fish Company. Throughout the day, elevator doors open and men bark "watch it, coming through." Postal workers push into the fourth-floor mailroom over 300 dirty gray pushcarts, each containing five plastic trays stacked with envelopes. Then temporarily employed students and pensioners pound the trays on long tables to drive the contents to the bottom of the envelopes, run them through Lightning Slicing Machines, and carry the opened envelopes to "extractors," women who are paid $70 a week.

These women—contrary to the myth that Internal Revenue's personnel scrutinize each envelope to detect people filing hours after the April 15 deadline—seldom look at postmarks except when a bellicose taxpayer forces their attention to it. Periodically an envelope is addressed "*Infernal* Revenue Service" with "Infernal" underlined; or contains a hand-drawn arrow that points to a postmark ("April 15, P.M.") with the notation: "Whee! I beat you." Otherwise the envelopes are dropped into a wastebasket.

(Later the envelopes are spread on a glass table, lit from underneath by a high-powered fluorescent bulb. This X-ray-like process determines whether or not anything remains inside.)

The extractors perfunctorily remove the envelopes' contents, staple checks and money orders to the returns, and when they occasionally find cash in an envelope, raise their hands to attract a supervisor who initials the return and delivers the money to the cashier. Next, extractors sort incoming returns into bins: the white, individual forms 1040 and 1040A with payment attached into one bin; individual returns without payment into a bin marked "non-remittance;" corporations' blue returns into a third bin; business partnerships' yellow forms in the next; and miscellaneous into a bin labeled "others." Afterwards, more young "temps," with a supervisor carefully following them, haul the returns in shopping carts to appropriate sections of the Wage and Excise Unit on the fifth floor.

Here other women, called Grade-5 examiners and paid about $100 a week, sit at long tables and scan returns for obvious errors. These returns are sent back to taxpayers with a form letter because they are unsigned, undecipherable, incomplete, fail to include Social Security number or Form W-2 listing wages earned and taxes withheld by employer. Examiners also search for checks that don't match the sum due on the return; and letters or marginal comments that accompany some returns. While most correspondence generally states why a person cannot pay at that time or if they are "paying too much then please return," there is plenty of sarcasm. Take the would-be

41

poet who, in 1963, wrote: "Once a year I get so blue because of that old Internal Revenue."

One taxpayer cryptically wrote: "Have tax to pay—no money—any suggestions?" Another note read: "I understand President Johnson has declared war on poverty. Please advise as to where I surrender." Possibly the rarest request came from the female who attached to her return a money order for unpaid taxes, $8 worth of Merchant's green stamps and this note: "Please send me an autographed picture of the district director of taxes."

Finally there are those persons seeking permission to file late. Requests that sound plausible usually are granted. Sometimes they are not so plausible. One man mailed a blank Form 1040 and this optimistic note: "Please grant me a 10-day extension on the April 15 deadline. I can't pay the taxes now but my horoscope said I will come into big money on the 25th and I will pay you then." Another man wrote: "As I was getting the blank tax forms out of the mailbox I was bitten by a black widow spider and I have been too sick to complete the return. I am not really accusing your office of sending the spider with the forms, but. . . ."

Letters, though, can—and do—wait. Returns accompanied by some form of payment, or applications for refund, must receive priority. First, all remittance returns are bundled in groups of 100 and carted to the Cashier's Section. Here 242 employees, mostly women, remove the checks and money orders, write the taxpayer's name and amount of payment on a yellow prenumbered form called "Remittance Register," then repeat the process on four other forms for cross-reference. After balancing clerks verify all arithmetic, the checks are sent through an automatic endorsing machine. At the end of a day, the total amount of receipts is written on an orange "Certificate of Deposit," which resembles an ordinary checking account deposit slip except for one fact: Daily deposits frequently total $250 million. And over a year, this section deposits $14.2 billion, giving the Manhattan District the nation's highest tax collections.

Next the slips, checks and currency are taken by armored car three blocks down the street and deposited at the Irving Trust Company. But like any organization that accepts personal checks, Internal Revenue is not immune to an old problem. "A bum check? We get up to 800 checks a day that bounce," explains the section chief, Mrs. Frances Isamisaic, a gray-haired woman with a big charm bracelet and 30 years' experience at Internal Revenue. "But we have the bank automatically redeposit the bouncers at least once before sending them back to us and it's waiting there if the taxpayer makes a deposit. A good many checks clear the second time around. If not, we add on the bounce penalty—1 percent of the amount due or a $5 minimum and bill them the same day. We don't take any more personal checks from these people either."

A comparable number of checks, though representing smaller amounts, also flow from Internal Revenue. Over half of all returns seek refunds for overpayment of taxes and receive equal attention during the processing stages.* Refund checks must be issued within 45 days from the April 15 filing deadline or Internal Revenue must pay 6 percent annual interest *even if the return was filed late.* The law (or loophole for late filers) forced IRS to pay

* The number of refund claims was much lower in 1965 due to the lower amounts withheld from paychecks.

interest of $88.5 million in 1964. Therefore the deadline also has necessitated that IRS pay many refund claims that were not exceptionally large, then check the records later to determine if the filer had a legitimate claim. Frequently he did not, leaving Internal Revenue highly vulnerable to swindlers, including one who filed an estimated 1,000 fictitious claims, each for $95.40. He received many of the refund checks until a suspicious postman reported that every day he delivered "dozens and dozens" of Internal Revenue's checks to "new" tenants in a small building. Even convicts, particularly those serving life sentences and unconcerned with receiving additional time, have developed hobbies of filling out phony refunds claims. Since prison addresses usually are a post-office box number, the returns initially create little suspicion at Internal Revenue Service. In the early 1960's, at least 101 convicts at California's Folsom prison were found to be receiving or seeking illegal tax-refund checks. Still no tax swindler displayed more brazenness, nor better illustrates Internal Revenue's predicament, than the Chicagoan who completed in the same handwriting 56 fictitious refund claims totaling $21,000. He received $15,585 before he was arrested, and while free on bail, kept receiving refund checks which he used to buy a new automobile.

But this problem is headed toward extinction. The new electronic computer system, Automatic Data Processing (ADP), will virtually eliminate chances of collecting fictitious refunds and at the same time revolutionize Internal Revenue's techniques. "ADP rescues us from damn near being at the mercy of unscrupulous operators and multiple filers," emphasizes Clinton Walsh, IRS' director of operation in charge of ADP. "Why before a jeweler could be dodging our agents to avoid paying his excise tax, but still file—and promptly collect—a $500 refund on his individual income taxes. Now we can verify the claim, eliminate multiple or duplicate filers, spot those who owe other past taxes, and issue legitimate refund checks well within the 45-day limit."

Significantly ADP will cause two other major changes in progressing everyone's tax return. One, it will transfer much of the voluminous clerical work and uncertain mathematical verification that IRS employees call "paper pushing" to digital computers. Two, ADP will, for the first time in Internal Revenue's history, create a master file on every taxpaying American individual or business and place them under the surveillance of centralized computers. All business returns have been scrutinized by the computers since 1965. Four-sevenths of the nation's individual returns had been programmed into the computers by January, 1966; the remainder in January, 1967.

Thus, instead of clerical workers at district offices tediously checking taxpayers' arithmetic and making adjustments, the sorted returns are shipped in locked canvas bags to one of seven regional service centers that have been built since 1963 in Ogden, Utah; Austin, Texas; Kansas City, Missouri; Chamblee, Georgia; Cincinnati, Ohio; Lawrence, Massachusetts; and Philadelphia, Pennsylvania. All seven centers use identical processing methods. Take the one in northeast Philadelphia. After returns are unloaded by hydraulic lifts at the cavernous, one-story white brick building, they are put through a machine that numbers them and then are wheeled on "batch carts" into the main room. The fluorescent-lit room, at first sight, is almost overwhelming and it's almost impossible to see

45

from one end to the other. It is equivalent in size to four football fields and has 2,600 employees, working in two shifts, sitting at gray tin desks or typewriterlike key punch machines.

Most of these employees, apart from the upper management level, are women. At least 1,600 are temporarily employed housewives, or young girls in their first job, who earn $70 a week, and are not tax experts, but females who have taken a 10-day course and still are not unmindful of coffee-break time, lunch time and quitting time. Consequently (and since the center is so immense) each employee must wear a blue, yellow or green tag that signifies at what time she may appear in the cafeteria or leave the building.

About 900 of these women are called Grade 2 or Grade 4 examiners and do what is called editing and coding. They read the returns and put a numerical code beside each figure. At the same time, the women also sift out 3.5 percent of the returns that still have problems such as illegibility or incompleteness and must be returned to the district office. The edited returns are then carted to the transcription area where over 900 other women sit and make about 55,000 key strokes a day on an IBM 24 Card Punch machine. In doing this work, the key punchers transfer all information on a short-form individual return to about 80 perforated positions on two 2½-by-6-inch cards. A more detailed return may require up to 16 cards.

After the cards are proofread by more women punching a No. 56 Card Verifier machine, they are taken into the glass-enclosed computer room and inserted, first into a No. 108 Card Proving machine that determines the amount of money listed on the cards and the total number of returns, and then into a grey IBM 188 that arranges the cards in numerical sequence. Now the cards are turned over to male technicians, mostly in their thirties and early forties, who operate six computer machines. Technicians feed the cards into a blue machine called a 12 K card reader that is connected to a bright blue Honeywell 200, or "memory unit," that decides how the cards must be programmed.

Then, with the computers adjusted accordingly, the cards are automatically fed at the rate of 650 per minute through a tape drive machine which reduces the average taxpayer's return to a half-inch of dots, invisible to the naked eye but recognizable by a digital computer as positive or negative electronic charges on a half-inch-wide brown metallic tape. Simultaneously the memory computer detects mathematical errors on one of every eight returns (a detection ratio three times higher than that of IRS's best human examiners) and records these and other problematic items on a separate error tape. Later that tape is fed into the 12K machine, which can be programmed for different jobs, and activates a console tele-printer to send a bill for additional taxes, a notification that there is a discrepancy in the information on the return, or eventually to send such grim messages as: FINAL NOTICE BEFORE SEIZURE (for unpaid taxes) or RE-QUEST FOR INFORMATION FROM EMPLOYERS TO LOCATE INDIVIDUAL (who obviously is hiding from Internal Revenue).

The 500 reels of perfect tape, each containing about 15,000 returns, are loaded into what employees call the Martinsburg station wagon. Meanwhile, 2,900 similar reels from Internal Revenue's six other service centers have been air expressed to Washington, D.C.'s National Airport, where messengers take the tapes 68 miles through the peaceful Shenandoah Valley to a new one-story brick building on Route 9 near Martinsburg, West Virginia. Outside a sign reads: NATIONAL COMPUTER CENTER. INTERNAL REVENUE SERVICE. Inside, past a belatedly constructed glass booth to accommodate tourists, sits the ballyhooed "central brain" or "Martins-burg Monster"—a 7074 IBM computer, two 360 IBM computers, and 25 other machines that were first rented at $7 million a year, then purchased from International Business Machines, Inc. (IBM).

An eerie feeling grips visitors as they tour the building, listening to a supervisory technician explain what is being done. It moves a few to recall George Orwell's *1984,* a shuddering novel about a superstate central government which shrank all humans into brainwashed numbers. This building, you see, contains neither the tax forms nor paper that seems synonymous with Internal Revenue's other offices. There are few persons visible: Only about 35 employees are needed on each of the 4 shifts that operate the computers 24 hours a day, 7 days a week. All anyone can see are silent machines and plastic canisters containing 1,000 miles of tape with people's names transformed into 9-digit numbers.

Every taxpaying American has been, by a 1961 Congressional Act, allocated a permanent number. Nearly 90 percent of these figures are Social Security numbers; the remainder are Employees Identification Numbers assigned to persons such as waiters and bartenders who are ineligible to participate in the Social Security program. Without numbers, full names and addresses are undigestible to the computers. Even before ADP was installed, the enormous number of identical names often precipitated unimaginable problems. "Look, there are nearly one and a half million taxpayers named Smith and thousands of John A. Smiths," points out Clinton Walsh, IRS's Director of Operations. "And there are 900,000 taxpaying Johnsons, 750,000 Williamses and 650,000 Browns. And one in every five changes his address each year. No telling how many get married. Many taxpayers would be unidentifiable without numbers."

No number, though, confuses the computers. The reels of numbered taxpayers' records then are inserted into one of 24 digital computers that sit in two L-shaped arrangements in a small, windowless room. One computer reassembles the returns in identifying numerical order and onto another reel. Now the tape is fitted either into the main 7074 or the 360 computers that compares the return with information whizzing through on *other* reels of half-inch tape that are labeled Individual Master File (IMF) and Business Master File (BMF). These master tapes contain the status of all taxpayers' previous two returns and where they were filed, his marital situation, number of dependents, and his reported income and any share of the $15 billion that is annually paid in dividends and interest and reported to Internal Revenue.*

* Still about 40 percent of the dividends and interest, representing $3.7 billion and $850 million in unpaid taxes, remains unreported. One survey indicates that many persons who opened savings accounts before Internal Revenue required them to furnish banks their social security number won't comply. Many, in order to conceal the bank account from wives, sign a "no mail" application so that banks cannot legally notify them to report their numbers. In Tulsa, Oklahoma, a savings and loan association said that it nevertheless notified such depositors and "lost quite a few savings accounts."

The computers' central mechanism, which is reading, comparing, adding and subtracting 680,000 characters per second, sails at astonishing speed past tax returns that include all reported income and are free of technical errors. At the same time, the computer issues its decisions on other returns through seven output tapes and, occasionally, a gray console typewriter. Take, for example, how the computers react to a particular return that seeks a refund. If the claim matches the overpayment that is recorded on the master tape and the taxpayer has no delinquent bills or erroneous arithmetic, the request appears on a refund tape that automatically writes refund checks when inserted into another computer at either of the Treasury's Disbursing offices in Philadelphia or Birmingham. If, however, a woman files a legitimate claim for a $55 refund and owes $80 in taxes from a previous year, the machine instead credits $55 to her account and lists her on a debit tape that later will bill her for $25, plus 6 percent annual interest. In 1965, the computer stopped payment on $33.6 million in legitimate refunds, which previously would have been issued, because the would-be recipients owed back taxes. The machines also prevented $3 million being paid for fictitious or erroneous refund applications.

When the robot encounters situations in refund claims, or on any return, in which it hasn't been programmed to make an automatic decision, it seeks help by directing the gray typewriter to print the taxpayer's number along with a code indicating an unexplainable discrepancy. On the morning of February 19, 1963, for example, the machine created a disturbance that quickly brought technicians on the midnight to 8 A.M. shift to the typewriter. Awed, they saw the Monster repeatedly print number 551-32-7319. Was the computer jammed on that numerical sequence? No. The Monster quickly added a code word that indicated it had caught its first multiple filer. Taxpayer No. 551-32-7319 had filed identical refund claims for $331.10 in 13 southern cities from Atlanta to Nashville.

The computer's potential, though restricted to what Internal Revenue personnel programs it to do, is said to be virtually limitless. In ADP's first full year of operation in the seven southeastern states, the 7074 computer detected 14,000 persons who didn't file a return, a task that would have been physically impossible by manual methods. It also found that taxpayers had overcharged themselves $72 million, others underpaid Internal Revenue by $165 million, giving the government upon payment a net gain of $93 million or an average of $1.47 per return. Moreover, after the robot has been "debugged," perfected and fully implemented, it can spot returns that are mathematically correct but will contain what it is adjusted to consider an unusual characteristic. It will, among other things, put a taxpayer's number on a suspicious list if:

His deductions for medical expenses exceed a limitation discreetly imposed by Internal Revenue.

A low-income person inherits his parents' home and his real estate taxes listed on the deductions depict him as living beyond his visible means.

A wife gives birth to twins (most certainly if triplets) and thus adds more than one $600 exemption to a couple's return in a single year (fictitious dependency deductions are the most common petty evasion scheme).

And much more. "Why the darn machine could spew out paper over the 50 states if we didn't control it," Bertrand Harding, Internal Revenue's deputy commissioner, has said. IRS does control the "Monster." Actually the computers select so many more possible discrepancies than Internal Revenue employees can process that technicians periodically adjust the machines to concentrate on more profitable targets.

The targets, when returns have reached this stage, are taxpayers who have been listed on output lists called "Audit-Select." These lists, along with all original tax returns, are sent to the appropriate district office. When both the lists and processed returns, arranged by income groups, arrive at the Manhattan District, for example, they are taken to a large, locked steel cage on the fifth floor. Here Jules Liberman, chief classifying officer, signs a receipt for the returns. Then he assigns the returns to Grade-11 classifiers, nearly all male revenue agents paid from $166 to $217 a week, to determine the returns' final status. These decisions, which may eventually disturb affected taxpayers, seem to concern even other Internal Revenue employees. One is Mrs. Elizabeth Sobkiewicz, a white-haired woman who joined Internal Revenue in 1936 as a temporary addressing-machine operator and advanced to chief of the Mail Room and Processing Section. Since Mrs. Sobkiewicz speaks authoritatively about much of the fourth and fifth floors' activities, she was asked, "What is the classifying section doing?" "I wouldn't dare ask and they wouldn't tell me if I did," she replied, shaking her head for emphasis. "Even if they would tell me, I just don't want to know. It's too secret."

What classifying agents do is this: They flip through returns, if time permits that much attention, and scribble "F" (file) on control cards of most short Form 1040A returns involving incomes under $10,000 or wages that are substantiated with a Form W-2. These returns are carted to a tightly guarded Index and Records File Section on the third floor where young girls stack them at a rate of 6,000 a day on open steel shelves. "And nobody except the filers and supervisors can go in the area and nobody can come here and see anybody's return," says Helen Duffy, the section chief and another of Internal Revenue's 32-year veterans. "The only time a return is pulled from here is when the agent brings in a Form 2275 that's been approved by his supervisor and states why the return is wanted."

Except for the returns that are pulled, no one ever sees them again. They remain on the shelves for three years before being "retired" and shipped to Federal Records Center warehouses in low rent areas.* Corporate returns remain indefinitely in the warehouses. But after individual returns are kept another three years, making them six years old, they are sold, without microfilming them, for pulp. (Each year the government's General Services Administration sells 750 tons of old tax returns for $2,000.)

Ultimately the classifiers examine the remaining bundles of returns and, on some, mark "SFA" (Selected For Audit) and grades of essentiality, such as "A-1," on the control cards and send them to the Audit Department on

* A statute of limitations prohibits assessing additional taxes three years after a return is filed unless fraud is involved. A new trend, however, makes it easier to suspect fraud. Twice in 1965, the Supreme Court held that Internal Revenue did not have to show reasonable cause for assuming fraud before compelling taxpayers to produce records for the closed years three to six years after the filing date. But argued Justice William Douglas, who dissented in both opinions: "The government should have to show more than mere caprice before it can investigate returns older than four years."

the 10th floor. A-1 is the highest priority grade and indicates that these returns must be audited first. A-1, or any grade of "SFA" means that most persons who filed these returns now face a new, nervewracking tax season that can extend from May to November.

4

The Dreaded Audit

Tax returns that contain a mathematical or technical error often bring the Internal Revenue Service's bill for additional taxes and a notice: "Your return has not been audited. If it is selected for audit, you will be contacted." Those contacted usually filed returns that indeed were mathematically correct. But the Internal Revenue Code's 1,000 pages of ambiguous definitions and 19,000 pages of exceptions, preferences and flexible rulings convert many honest taxpayers into angle-seekers and fertilize other individuals' imaginations when filling out their returns. Interpretation of the Code also furnishes the Service a broad longitude. After an audit, IRS can, among many alternatives, disallow claimed deductions that are not substantiated with written receipts; decide that business expenses involved personal motives, not "ordinary and necessary business expense"; or rule that an exception is not applicable in that case.

This perennial chance of being audited also encourages

some restraint in filling out returns. Therefore a few individuals at IRS have not exactly discouraged the notion that the Service audits almost all returns, although it still is physically impossible to do so even with the computers' assistance. Illustrative is the lead of a public-service article under then-Commissioner Mortimer Caplin's byline:*

It is probably prophetic that, when I became commissioner of Internal Revenue in 1961, I was in the middle of a three year tax audit. In fact, an Internal Revenue man was in my office going over my returns when Andrew Hatcher of the late President Kennedy's White House staff telephoned to say my appointment was about to be announced. When I hung up the phone, the agent glanced at me quizzically. He had heard enough of the conversation to know what had happened. "I feel a little silly," he said, "examining the books of my new boss." Then he rustled the tax forms. "But about this 1960 return—I still think I'll have to see more proof before I can allow this deduction."

Thus "you" too will probably face such an audit, Caplin continued buoyantly. "You," as a taxpayer, face no more than a 20 to 1 chance of being completely audited, since only 3.15 million of the 65.5 million individual tax returns and 350,000 of the remaining 37 million corporation, business, excise, estate, gift and miscellaneous returns were audited in 1965. Neither is everyone susceptible to genuine spot checks such as auditing all taxpayers whose surname begins with "C" or every tenth return in Chicago. Essentially, five factors cause a return to be audited, whether the decision is made by a computer, classifying officer or auditor:

A return that has itemized deductions and claims a

* *Family Weekly,* March 29, 1964.

large refund for an overpayment of taxes instead of apply-
ing it toward the next year's tax bill receives what is
called the "pre-refund audit." The reasoning for this,
maintains an assistant Internal Revenue commissioner,
Robert Jack, is "that it's easier for us to examine the return
and correct obvious mistakes than to refund the overpayment then go back later and try to recover the money." If
an Audit Division has a large inventory of returns to be
examined, it will temporarily omit audits of returns claiming a refund under $100, then, if it catches up, resume,
say, a $25 or $50 limit tolerance.

Most individual returns will be selected for audit if it
is noticed that they claim certain amounts or types of
deductions. The most common reason for auditing a return is that it deducted more than 14 percent (sometimes
less) of the reported income for unidentified medical
expenses, charitable contributions and interest on a home
mortgage. The next category is taking $600 exemptions
for dependents other than wives or children (such as
mothers and aunts); deductions for casualties, such as
wrecked automobiles and flooded homes; and unprofitable
secondary occupations involving subjects like dogs,
horses, farming or writing and possibly a hobby. Individuals invite audits if they report high gross and low net
incomes; claim an automobile was used entirely for business; or list substantial expenses for travel and entertainment.

Heavy emphasis is given self-employed persons who
deal largely in currency and whose income, therefore,
cannot be verified by employers or computers. And for apt
reason: The highest ratio of underreporting income is

among motel and beauty-parlor operators, doctors and dentists, all of whom keep their own records of income; and lawyers and accountants, whose dealings with tax cases often enable them to partially learn (and challenge) Internal Revenue's imperfect system of catching tax evaders.

Apart from organized criminals, whom the Department of Justice tries to convict on tax law violations, certain individuals are almost invariably audited because of their history of tax evasion, suspicious deductions, or having been reported as "tax evaders" by informers (informers are described in the next chapter).

What generally is called "spot checks" actually means examining individuals or businesses solely because they have a high income. The chance of being audited ranges from near zero for low income groups up to 100 percent for the high income category. IRS audits only about 1.95 million of the 56.1 million taxpayers whose incomes are classified as "low" (under $10,000),* but audits 1.1 million of the 9.4 million taxpayers whose incomes are categorized as "medium low" ($10,000 to $29,999), "medium high" ($30,000 to $49,000) and "large" (above $50,000). Approximately half of the persons in these income classifications file returns that take the minimum standard deduction or are accompanied by Forms W-2 that verify salary paid and taxes withheld, leaving almost no practical reason for an audit. Thus IRS audits nearly one of every three remaining taxpayers and, where incomes exceed $50,000, audits almost every one. The Service also

---

* After adjustments for personal exemptions, 13 million of the 56.1 million "low" incomes are so low—under $500 for individuals or $1,000 for married couples—that such persons pay no income taxes.

automatically audits 333,000 corporation and large business accounts each year.

What happens when returns are transferred to the District Offices' Audit Divisions is this: They are placed in steel cabinets labeled "Unassigned Selected Returns" and periodically removed by group supervisors. Returns involving incomes under $10,000 or minor deductions usually are allotted to young Grade-5 examiners, mostly men and women trained in accounting or business administration. The complex returns are processed by more experienced G-7 or G-9 auditors. All examiners and auditors work in groups of 15 at closely bunched steel desks, monotonously read figures and occasionally chuckle and call the nearest person's attention to deductions like those listed by one traveling salesman. His business expenses included: "39 trips to pay toilet, @ 10¢—total $3.90." Still, examiners know that distracting deductions, especially if listed early on a return, frequently are bait to camouflage other fictitious expenses. A case in point was a minister, apparently gambling that auditors would stop upon detecting one error, who listed a $2.37 clerical collar under business deductions as "$237." Auditors found that return (plus two earlier returns) contained several implausible expenses.

This preliminary review determines which of the three auditing systems will be used. The simplest method is the correspondence audit in which a taxpayer is sent a form letter asking him to identify or mail "substantiation" for the deduction that is checked. A coded envelope is provided in order that the reply bypasses Internal Revenue's mailroom and travels directly to the Audit Division. Here a group clerk files the taxpayer's correspondence or receipts into that person's manila folder. Eventually the audit group will review that answer, along with about 300 other replies a day, to decide if the questioned deduction is allowed, attach a report to the return, and give it to the supervisor to initial. Then a taxpayer's canceled checks are returned either if he is charged additional tax and interest or sent a form letter that his return is "accepted as filed." Often, if there are no receipts to return, the taxpayer is billed for additional taxes and interest without any discernible explanation why his deduction was denied. If the taxpayer telephones, he usually is advised to pay (the bill states he must pay within 10 days) and write a letter, which, in turn, takes another two or three months for a reply.

Though IRS's exchange of correspondence annoys some and frightens others, it brings out an earthy frankness in many persons. Specifically, a tavern owner, asked how he justified claiming his automobile as a business expense, replied: "How else can I get drunks home?" A farmer, told to "advise the method of depreciation and disposition of your second-hand truck," answered: "If this truck had a disposition, it was mean and ornery." None was more concise than the man who explained a casualty loss deduction this way: "Woman driver in front of me. *Left* turn signal blinking, made *right* turn. Cr-r-runch! Auto loss claim: $200."

Not all ostensibly funny replies have hilarious endings. On the West Coast, a female tax examiner's intuition was aroused by another female's explanation of a $50 casualty loss: "I am considered very statuesque and a new $50 bikini was ripped from my body and completely destroyed while I was at the beach." The examiner took the time to check the alleged beauty's previous two tax returns and found the claim had been made for three consecutive years. She had to pay 19 percent tax and 6 percent interest on the $150 that had been deducted.

The most detailed examinations are field audits that occur at businesses or offices of individuals with voluminous records. Audit teams, usually a certified public accountant and three less-experienced examiners, work full time on tax returns of corporations such as United States Steel, which in fiscal 1965, paid $235 million in federal taxes.* On this level, audits are orderly but intricate. An audit team maintains desk space at U.S. Steel's office at 71 Broadway, meets with the corporation's accountants, pores arduously over records, and attempts to resolve differences there. Frequently, decisions are made in advance. Today Internal Revenue's position on how it would tax a transaction often dictates whether or not many corporations will finalize certain business. Hence each year IRS's technical staff issues over 35,000 written rulings on how it would react to a hypothetical situation: Yes (or No), U.S. Steel, the acquisition and disposition of the assets, after being held more than six months, qualifies as a long-term capital gain (and therefore taxable at a rate of 25 percent instead of corporations' highest tax rate of 48 percent). A single ruling can involve millions and millions of dollars in taxes. As Roger Blough, U.S. Steel's board chairman reported on a tax ruling at a stockholders' meeting in 1965: If we exchange all outstanding preferred stock for 4 5/8 percent debentures (a debt security) we can save about $10 million in taxes. Why? Interest on debentures can be

* The nation's leading taxpayer is General Motors, which paid taxes of $2.5 billion in fiscal 1965 and still made a profit of $2.1 billion.

deducted from taxable income while stock dividends are nondeductible. Stockholders, of course, voted for the tax savings.

Even rulings unfavorable to the corporations are highly systematized. Since 6 percent interest is added to taxes that go unpaid after 90 days from assessment, most corporations pay what IRS auditors levy, then, if its accountants feel that Internal Revenue erred, claim a refund or sue to recover the money. For example, in 1964–65, such huge corporations as U.S. Steel, Standard Oil of New Jersey, Radio Corporation of America and Time, Inc., sued Internal Revenue for refunds up to $30 million each on grounds that auditors erred in disallowing deductions or exemptions. (Evidently, relations aren't, as IRS auditors maintain, damaged by such suits. When International Business Machines, or IBM, learned that Internal Revenue's auditors had erroneously ruled in a letter to Remington Rand Corporation that the sale or lease of certain computers was not subject to excise taxes, IBM sued and won an $11 million refund from Internal Revenue for taxes paid on similar computers during a period when IRS was leasing enough computers to be one of IBM's best customers. In 1966, the Supreme Court upheld the refund.)

An entirely different approach often is used at smaller businesses. Sometimes two-man audit teams arrive unannounced at a stockbroker's or doctor's office, inspect all receipts, canceled checks and occasionally persuade stenographers to give them other records not intended for Internal Revenue's use. Surprisingly, some professional men who underreport their income to IRS also maintain, perhaps moved by ego, another accurate record of their income. Therefore IRS field auditors have been known to spend long hours analyzing records, sometimes even breaking a code. Take the doctor who reported an income of $10,000 but whose living style suggested an income of $40,000. Each audit matched his reported income and the total amount listed on the patients' case history cards. Ultimately auditors detected a pattern to several tiny dots and dashes under a patient's name. Each dot represented to the doctor that he had not reported $5, a dash signified $10 had been concealed, and three dashes and a dot indicated $35 in unreported income.

Field auditors also appear, though usually by appointment, at the premises of the wealthy and often aim at a particular target: contributions. These auditors have learned from experience and instructions to mistrust frequently receipts for charitable gifts even when they are signed by a curator or preacher. Since Internal Revenue taxes 70 percent of an individual's income above $200,000, some wealthy persons transfer themselves into a lower tax bracket when they give property to churches, schools, hospitals, museums or foundations. The recipient hands the donator a receipt and the latter, of course, deducts the amount listed from his taxable income. But as Commissioner Sheldon Cohen says: "Certain institutions encourage people to make contributions in terms of works of art with sort of a shading of the value or looking the other way to encourage the gift and this is not correct." Internal Revenue's attitude on any type of large contribution can be illustrated by the Chicago District office's handling of two cases. One woman donated household goods and clothing that had been appraised at $5,500 to a hospital, then deducted $5,500 from her taxable income. IRS auditors found that the hospital had auctioned the gift for $450. The same hospital a month later received the contents of a 14-room apartment on Chicago's elegant Lake Shore Drive that had been appraised at approximately the retail price of $62,073, but was auctioned for $6,620. Once more IRS rejected the deduction for the contribution's appraised value, and the donator had to go to court to obtain a deductible claim of $15,200. (Incidentally, not *all* of the 268 taxpayers whose annual incomes exceed a million dollars overload their tax form's Part IV with charitable contributions. In one recent year, a millionaire claimed only $100 a year for charity; two deducted under $200 and five millionaires listed under $500. The 268 taxpaying millionaires averaged donations of $333,238, or 17 percent, of their income.)

The third category, involving about 75 percent of the examined returns, is called the office audit. During the peak audit season of June through October the taxpayer is mailed a Notice of Examination, which orders the person to report at a certain time at IRS's district office to justify the items checked on the form letter. Invariably this letter suggests something catastrophic to most recipients. Taxpayers told to reply by letter obviously can see that Internal Revenue doesn't need to interrogate them. High-income individuals and businessmen expect the field auditors each year. But because of man's fear of the unknown, an ordinary taxpayer expects the worst if he has to appear at Internal Revenue headquarters. After all, he has been thoroughly exposed to grim news of tax evaders drawing prison sentences. Usually he doesn't know that, *unless* he has deliberately and willfully underreported more than 25 percent of his income or claimed fictitious dependents, his penalty simply will be 6 percent interest on any extra tax that is assessed. Too, the prospect of having to pay more taxes is not very pleasant.

Consequently, a few taxpayers, like the myth, even wear old clothing to feign poverty. Notably one extremist, a miser who was found to owe $80,000 in taxes and penalties, wore a rope to hold up his pants. Another frightened man brought in a bouquet of faded artificial flowers that he had bought on street corners from nonprofitable organizations which, he said, documented his charitable deductions. A woman carried in three shopping bags filled with empty medicine bottles and a 25-cent spiral notebook containing notations that she had swallowed 16,332 pills over a number of years.

Then there are the few spunky protestors like the man in Detroit who had filled out his return in Roman numerals and then insisted the Internal Revenue examiner use (which he did) only such figures during the audit. Perhaps the noisiest complainer was a thin man in a plaid sport coat who said Internal Revenue unfairly "corralled him" and, in reprisal, left three feet of heavy metal Cyclone fence in the Manhattan District office's audit waiting room.

At the same Manhattan office, however, it is apparent that appearing for an audit is about as pleasant as reporting at 5:30 A.M. at an Army induction center. The smaller taxpayer, usually a male wearing a sport coat and appearing alone, and the more affluent, accompanied by an accountant carrying a monogrammed briefcase, both step off the elevator on the 10th floor and hand their Form 3421 letter to one of two middle-aged female receptionists. She stamps the letter in a time clock, then spins and hands it through a slot in the glass partition to girls called searchers. A searcher thumbs through an open bin, called a File-o-Graph, that always contains from 10,000 to 30,000 returns, locates that particular return and hands it and the Form 3421 to an assignment clerk. The clerk assigns the return to one of the 157 examiners, who then studies it for about five minutes.

Meanwhile, the taxpayer sits in one of seven rows of modern plastic chairs in a light blue waiting room that extends into the hallway. Most of the people, one afternoon in October of 1965, had near-identical solemn expressions; eyes moved searchingly toward anyone leaving the audit room. It seemed reminiscent of schoolchildren awaiting a vaccination and silently asking: "Did it hurt much?" (Once a plump woman emerged from the audit section and did advise, "It didn't hurt a bit!") None of these people spoke to each other. One middle-aged man in a shiny black coat quietly removed a gold watch and slid it into a pocket. A woman, about 30 and wearing a raincoat over a nurse's uniform, tried to pull off what appeared to be a sapphire ring, frowned, then walked to the water fountain, slid her finger under the cold stream, helping to ease off the ring.

A stocky man wearing a brown sport coat and no tie had waited about 30 minutes. Then a clean-shaven male examiner, about 28 years old, appeared and announced: "Mr. Barker?" The man followed the examiner to a glass-partitioned cubicle and sat down at one of two steel desks that are purposely bare. The first thing the examiner mentioned was the pleasant Indian summer day. It is possible to surmise the conversation because such procedures are standardized. Examiners have explicit instructions from the Office Audit Chief, Peter Dillon, a stout, crew-cut ex-field auditor in his early forties. "Don't even have a book on your desk," he tells them. "If a taxpayer you hit hard sees a Kennedy book he's gonna complain that you hate Republicans. If you try to be nice and mention the World Series, he's liable to say you wasted two hours of his time discussing the Dodgers. Limit any side talk to the weather—the rain, the sleet or the sun. And don't give the taxpayer a chance to say you're dishonest because you didn't look him in the eyes. Look right at him and be courteous."

The stipulated congeniality, however, does not appeal to all audited taxpayers. One man, who will remain nameless, recalls his experience this way: "The examiner kept smiling and chuckling softly like I was a clever devil even though I'd said nothing that could be interpreted as funny. I guess it was to relax me. Then, quickly, he asked me to substantiate the $1,350 medical bill. My wife'd had a baby and we'd both had teeth fixed and I didn't have Blue Cross. So I had plenty of receipts from the hospital and doctors. He nodded and then said: 'This $120 for drugs. How much toothpaste and cigars did you buy at the drugstore?' "

Such prickly questioning, whether it involves an individual or business, office or field audit, distills to one point—prove it. The auditor often insists that the taxpayer prove the amount was spent and, if it involved a business lunch, what was discussed? While the auditor often will emphasize the taxpayer's honesty isn't being questioned, he simultaneously implies that the return is less than 100 percent correct (which it often is). If, for example, a married man being audited has claimed his automobile was used entirely for business, the examiner will usually ask: "Oh, you didn't use it on the 4th of July weekend? The vacation? Your wife never drives it?"

When a taxpayer is questioned about a casualty loss, such as a fire, storm or flood damaging a home, the examiner often asks: "What proof do you have?" If a taxpayer says he paid a bill in cash, the auditor will ask: "Why cash? Then how can you substantiate this?"

If a taxpayer is being questioned about charitable contributions, he often is challenged on any annual total above $78—a maximum calculated at giving $1 a week to a church or synagogue and 50 cents a week to door-to-door and street-corner can shakers. Still, if the examiner doubts the taxpayer's $78 deduction he sometimes will ask him to prove that he attended church to claim even the $52.*

While such interrogation often provokes conscientious taxpayers, it also detects some accidental and deliberate tax avoiders. Occasionally a man who has claimed an aunt as a dependent admits he gives her only "$10 every now and then." A few taxpayers include nondeductible items such as funeral expenses in medical deductions and losses from church-sponsored bingo games as charitable contributions. Or, as one woman admitted, her "business fees" were expenses for confession magazines and dues to lonely-hearts clubs, but she defended them with: "Well, they ought to be deductible. I'm trying to find myself a dependent husband." Sometimes, too, auditors encounter individuals who cannot distinguish between business and

---

* "If the churches received only 20 percent of the contributions listed on tax returns, churches would be rich," maintains Harold R. All, Commissioner of IRS's North Atlantic Region.

vacations. In one such case, an auditor and his supervisor disallowed a language professor's deduction of $1,300 for a two-month trip to Europe to perfect his skill as a linguist on grounds that it was a vacation. IRS's decision eventually was upheld by a federal judge who noted that the professor's expenses included books about sex and diets and that half of the trip was spent on the French Riviera, including an island known primarily for its nudist colony.

Since legitimate business and pleasure frequently do overlap, this complicates many auditors' decisions. Most examiners scrutinize expense accounts—a fact-of-life that they do not experience and are taught to suspect during their eight weeks of instruction and 20 weeks of on-job training. First, the G-5 examiner, if married, usually can afford no more than $10 a week for bus fare or parking, lunch, cigarettes and an occasional paper container of coffee. Not surprisingly, IRS regulations forbid him from accepting a complimentary lunch in order to avoid a possible conflict of interest. Yet he must decide if $17.50 claimed for a business lunch and drinks at Toots Shor's bar constitutes "ordinary and necessary" business, or pleasure.

Secondly, most examiners have read Internal Revenue's 1961 report called "Limited Audit Study—For Official IRS Use Only"—that says, in effect, that 85 percent of large travel and entertainment expenses are inflated. In that study of 100,000 returns with large expense accounts, IRS disallowed 48 percent, or $28.3 million of the amount claimed for expenses, and assessed $11.1 million in additional taxes because, it ruled, the deductions represented personal motives or couldn't be documented. Internal

Revenue was particularly austere on expenses that overlap with pleasure: It disallowed 93 percent of the deductions involving yachts or boats; 92 percent for club dues; 89 percent spent for farms; 85 percent for hunting areas, and 71 percent spent at conventions. Internal Revenue's conclusion had been previously supported by the findings of the House Committee on Ways and Means: "One of the most flagrant sources of inequity and corruption has been found in the inadequacies of existing record-keeping requirements . . . it has become clear from the investigation that under present law, exorbitant, unsubstantiated deductions have frequently been claimed."

The law under which Internal Revenue functioned was the so-called Cohan rule. The Supreme Court, in upholding songwriter-impresario George M. Cohan's deduction of $22,000 claimed to have been spent on entertainment to promote his Broadway plays, ruled that Internal Revenue must accept the taxpayer's reasonable estimate of expenses when records didn't exist. Subsequently, IRS received legislation in 1962 that shifted the burden of proof for travel and entertainment expenditures to the taxpayer by compelling him to furnish receipts for expenses above $25.

For another matter, tax examiners' careers are at stake. The Grade-5 examiners, who handle most office and routine audits, start at a salary of $5,181 a year and realize that if their work is favorably reviewed, they can advance to G-7, eventually G-9 and, perhaps in 10 or 12 years, to a G-11 revenue agent. Aside from being the status positions among IRS's working level, the agents' annual salaries range from $8,560 to $11,305. Therefore ambitious examiners attend night school and study training booklets such as Internal Revenue's "Effective Revenue Writing" ("be brief . . . People want quick, easily absorbed jets of meaning. Witness the style of *The Reader's Digest*"). Still an overriding criterion of the auditors' work is the amount of revenue produced, or what auditors are known to call "batting averages" and "revenue yield." Internal Revenue's group supervisors cannot be (and are not) expected to differ from, say, insurance executives who give comparable lists of prospects to two agents. One man sells ten policies, the other didn't make a sale but claims everyone was impressed with the quality of presentation. Anyone can *not* produce. Group supervisors want examiners on their team who don't lose all arguments, and, resultantly, lower their "revenue yield."

The reason for this is simply money. Admittedly, Internal Revenue is a giant collection agency and examiner-auditors are employed, though IRS denies it, to extract legally additional revenue from tax returns. In 1965, all of IRS's Audit Divisions assessed $2.72 billion, or an average of $777 per return examined, in extra taxes and interest. And Internal Revenue produces such sums, as former Commissioner Mortimer Caplin has told the House Appropriation Subcommittee in justifying its budget request, "by auditing returns that are the most profitable [for IRS] . . . higher income tax returns are . . . more productive."

In such unpublicized appearances before the House Subcommittee, IRS's top echelon personnel are candid about auditors' "yield" system. On March 22, 1966, Commissioner Sheldon Cohen even used two charts called "AVERAGE DOLLARS PER EXAMINATION" and "INCREASING YIELD PER MAN YEARS" to emphasize to

71

Congressmen that IRS auditors' average annual "yield" had dramatically increased from $125,885 in 1962 to $184,433 in 1966—and thus produced an average of $7.5 dollars in extra taxes for every dollar spent for auditors' salaries. As the Commissioner's prepared statement pointed out: "Notice that, in 1965, each office audit yielded (on the average) $89, but each field audit averaged $3,293. The chart also shows the remarkable increase since 1962 in the yield per examination field audit. Average additional tax recommended per field audit has jumped from $2,060 in 1962 to $3,293 in 1965 and is expected to go to $3,483 in 1967. That's an increase of 69 percent in 6 years, better than 10-percent increase a year. . . . A man-year spent on examining 77 corporation returns will yield (on the average) $590,000. The same man-year spent on examining 145 individual returns with AGI [adjusted gross incomes] under $10,000 will yield $125,000."

These statistics were not intended for public consumption because Internal Revenue has contended that (1) it prohibits IRS personnel from maintaining any such statistics, (2) the quota or "yield" system no longer exists, and (3) auditors are judged on their ability to perform a "blue ribbon" quality audit instead of the amount of additional revenue that they produce. No such denials of the quota system's existence, though, have been as hypocritical as those expounded by then-Commissioner Caplin. After announcing that he personally abolished the quota system, Caplin added that auditing tax returns is purely a moral obligation: "We do not audit returns for the purpose of making additional assessments. We examine returns to see if the tax laws have been obeyed."

But some of Manhattan's accounting firms so strongly contend that a comparable quota system is practiced by many auditors even if unofficially, that they have advised men in high-income brackets who face an annual audit to take precautions. Contending that most auditors invariably disallow at least a few deductions and assess some extra taxes, these men are said to deliberately add a few unsubstantiated deductions. Thus, when the auditor levies additional tax, the individual ends up paying about what he would have in the first place.

The percentage of those who pay—and thereby increase IRS's "revenue yield"—is high. Three of every five persons who appear before an IRS office examiner or auditor are asked to sign Form 870 that amends their original tax return and agrees that they owe additional taxes and interest. Does this three out of every five ratio exist because Internal Revenue's auditors maintain a quota system or because we largely are a nation of tax delinquents? As so often happens, the answer lies somewhere in the middle.

The National Office contends that examiners are instructed to "collect only the taxes that are due" and, while unable to deviate from basic tax laws, are allowed flexibility to meet local economic conditions. To illustrate, Manhattan's district can allow each taxpayer up to $78 in unproven charitable contributions, a sum that would neither be considered average nor permitted in, say, Appalachia. Furthermore, IRS statistics show that most auditors don't defy tax laws where they have no leeway. In 1965, IRS auditors did correct obvious errors—such as someone using the wrong tax table—and recommended that $145 million be returned to about 14 percent of all taxpayers who are audited. To assure that these and other recommendations are technically accurate, all audit reports are read by a supervisor and a reviewer. Then to prevent recurrent errors, the National Office distributes a bimonthly Audit Co-Ordination Digest that points out auditors' most common mistakes.

Yet the National or Regional offices' well-intentioned theories and what transpires at all collection and audit levels sometimes differ as much as a politician's campaign promises and what he produces in office. Though the proportion of conscientious employees in Internal Revenue's audit divisions is probably as high as in any government agency, there still is a noticeable incidence of IRS employees who disallow legitimate deductions and appear evidently unaware of some new (and old) interpretations. Cases of IRS officers arbitrarily denying legal deductions —often after the taxpayer previously had telephoned or written IRS and been told that an expense was deductible —are repeatedly told in letters to congressmen and newspapers. The complaints became so numerous in 1964, as the New Direction's crusade reached its vertex, that *Changing Times,* the Kiplinger magazine, suggested: "STICK UP FOR YOUR RIGHTS." "Some [tax] agents," the advisory publication said, "are just ornery . . . so don't knuckle under the threats . . . don't be browbeaten." An equally blunt criticism came in 1966 from the Commerce Clearing House's publication, *Taxes,* in a report entitled "HOW FAR CAN YOU TRUST A REVENUE AGENT?" and listing cases of IRS officials deciding a ruling one way on an issue only to have an auditor rule differently. In one such case that reached the U.S. Tax

Court, a judge even declared: "Harsh as it may be, one accepts the advice of a Revenue official at his peril."

Generally, there are several common areas of complaint:

1. The Internal Revenue Code clearly allows anyone whose business requires that he use an automobile to either itemize and substantiate actual expenses incurred or deduct 10 cents a mile up to 15,000 miles and 7 cents a mile thereafter without submitting receipts. Yet a few auditors refuse to allow businessmen to deduct 10 cents a mile unless they have receipts.

2. Auditors repeatedly refuse to allow anyone who must conduct out-of-town business to include the cost of meals on his deductible expense unless the person spent at least a night in a hotel or motel. Yet district, appeals and federal courts have ruled that the Internal Revenue Code allows such a deduction.

3. Federal Courts have ruled that a person may deduct as medical expense (if the sum exceeds 3 percent of a taxpayer's adjusted gross income) the entire premium for a hospitalization policy that pays both medical and weekly living expenses in event of illness. Tax auditors will allow only the portion of the premium paid for medical expense.

4. New York's IRS auditors, whom tax accountants maintain are the most rigid, allow taxpayers required to buy books for a business to deduct the cost over a number of years. Yet in South Carolina, the president of a small women's college was not allowed to deduct the cost of books on educational administration. Although the college president knew that his expense was legally deductible, he angrily wrote to the *New York Times*, his college's

board of directors advised that he not risk antagonizing IRS by appealing the decision.

Only a small percentage of individuals whose deductions are disallowed, whether right or wrong, *do* use existing systems to challenge IRS auditors. Why not? "The small taxpayer's first and usually last impulse is to quit," says Senator Warren Magnuson of Washington. "Just throw in the towel, pay the deficiency, no matter how unjust he believes it is, rather than face the tiers of faceless bureaucracy. The small taxpayer is faced with staggering disadvantages in his dealings with the Federal Government in comparison with large, corporate taxpayers." Furthermore, the upshot of such appeals, mostly by corporations and individuals who can afford lawyers and accountants, indicate that some IRS auditors seldom give taxpayers the benefit of a doubt. Approximately 10 percent of the individuals and businesses assessed additional taxes request an "informal conference" with the auditor's supervisor—and about half of those who take this step win some concession. Anyone who loses the argument is then allowed 30 days to pay the tax and interest before more interest is added. But in 1965, for example, 26,301 corporate and individual taxpayers—or 1 percent of those assessed with additional taxes—took their case to Internal Revenue's autonomous Appellate Division. Eighty-five percent of the disputes that reach this division are settled there for approximately $200 million a year less than what Internal Revenue had originally assessed. Anyone who doesn't want to sign Form 870AD, agreeing to pay the tax within 90 days, can sue. At this stage, IRS often maintains, "the door is open for settlement." (The door, incidentally, opens a little wider—occasionally it opens all the way and the case is dropped—when Internal Revenue's chief counsel feels it would have a weak case in court.)

Each year an average of 8,500 disagreements between IRS and taxpayers reach the courts, predominantly the U.S. Tax Court. While located in a wing of the IRS National Office building in Washington, the independent U.S. Tax Court is reasonably accessible to taxpayers. The Court has 22 judges who hear disputes all over the nation and it requires that taxpayers (though most complainants are represented by an attorney) merely type a letter-like brief stating the Revenue Code's provision that they feel entitles them to an exemption, then pay a $10 fee. Four out of five cases that reach Tax Court are settled without trial for only 31 percent of the amount that Internal Revenue had initially demanded.

In cases that have gone to trial, for example, the Tax Court has overruled IRS and upheld a man's medical deduction of $1,335 for a garage close to his home because the man's doctor ordered that he minimize walking on an injured leg. And the Court has even allowed a psychiatrist's own expense for psychoanalysis to treat his neurosis so that he could apply for admission to a school for psychoanalytical training. Still the Court is no lenient refuge for tax avoiders. It has, among many rulings, supported Internal Revenue's rejection of a $900 medical deduction for low-carbohydrate diet foods on grounds that the food replaces normal foods that would have ordinarily been consumed. Neither has the Court, like IRS auditors, symbolized consistency. The Tax Court's judges have repeatedly denied claims that yachts or racing boats are "necessary" business expenses while upholding some expenditures for the exotic safari. In a classic contradiction, the Court ruled that the president of Sanitary Farms Dairy of Erie, Pennsylvania, could deduct $16,443 for a six-month African safari, plus stopovers in Rome and Paris, on reasoning that the man and his wife subsequently showed movies of their travels and thereby advertised the dairy.

Theoretically, the U.S. Tax Court was established to give taxpayers a legal recourse and to interpret complex situations, thereby setting a judicial precedent. However, while Internal Revenue must follow the Tax Court's decision (unless reversed in a higher court) in any particular case, its policymakers often will not allow district auditors to apply the Tax Court's decision in similar cases. Nor will IRS always accept a legal precedent established by a state, district, federal or appeals court on contention that the ruling fits only that one case. Sometimes, of course, this is true. More often it is not. Three federal courts have separately ruled, for instance, that damage to an uninsured home caused by termites within a 15-month period could qualify as a tax-deductible casualty since the loss was sudden. Though forced to yield in those three cases, Internal Revenue steadfastly maintains that termites cannot eat away a house's foundation within two years and therefore the damage is not a casualty loss. Even "Your Federal Income Tax," an IRS publication that sells for 50 cents and is meant to interpret laws for taxpayers, states: "Termite damage is not a casualty loss." Such decisions motivated Senator John Sparkman of Alabama, chairman of the Select Committee on Small Business, to introduce a bill, S. 379, that would require IRS to follow the latest court decisions in its rulings. Though the bill wasn't enacted, three other congressmen afterwards sponsored similar legislation.

Moreover, another bill was aimed at partially softening the nuisance caused some taxpayers needlessly caught in the audit cycle. First, though, it should be acknowledged that the Audit Division's work goes entirely unappreciated. Second, an audit often is called "harassment" by many would-be tax avoiders. Yet each year Internal Revenue's bureaucratized auditing system does irritate thousands of honest taxpayers like the machinist in Milwaukee whom we'll call Walter Watson. Watson's ordeal began in August of 1957, when his wife excitedly telephoned him at work to say that they might be in "tax trouble." The Internal Revenue Service had sent a letter, Mrs. Watson said, that had an "X" beside the word "exemptions" and ordered him to report to the Milwaukee district office and substantiate that particular item. When the designated day arrived, the machinist left work at noon, changed clothing, and drove to IRS's district office. The tax examiner said that Watson would have to prove that he, and not any other relative, solely supported his mother before he could claim her as a $600 personal exemption. The examiner accepted Watson's documentation and said "the exemption's o.k. now."

Next year, however, Watson again was summoned before IRS's Audit Division to verify the same exemption. When the machinist said, "I proved this last year," the examiner, a different man and obviously unaware of Watson's previous documentation, stared innocuously and said he still needed proof. Watson supplied the evidence and the examiner said that the case was closed. In 1961, the machinist was subjected to the same ritual for the same exemption. In 1963, Watson again was ordered to an Internal Revenue office. "Surely," he thought, "it can't be the same damn thing." To find out, Watson telephoned the IRS office and was advised to follow the letter's instructions and report for the audit. Again Watson endured questions about supporting his mother and, as usual, the tax examiner knew nothing about any prior explanation. Finally in 1964 Watson was ordered to Milwaukee's IRS Audit Division for the fifth time in seven years. Exasperated, he wrote to his congressman. Normally such letters are forwarded with a note from the congressman's administrative assistant to the agency in question and bring an abstract response that the alleged injustice, if it exists, will be corrected. But this congressman, Henry S. Reuss, found that Watson's plight was additional support for his bill, H.R. 4273, to create an Administrative Counsel of Congress that would investigate citizens' complaints to members of Congress alleging that they have been abused by any federal agency, including the Internal Revenue Service. Representative Reuss's intervention brought a promise from the IRS district office to stop pestering Watson. The move also drew IRS's explanation that the problem originated from an inadequate data-retrieval system, a euphemism for five persons' failure to check its files to see if the exemption already had been substantiated.

Internal Revenue's officers are cognizant of this problem and have taken some remedial steps. Eventually, they maintain, the fact that a taxpayer has proven a perennial exemption can be noted on his computerized master file and the following year he will be bypassed when returns are selected for audit. This program already is used in two of the nation's seven regions and, according to an IRS statement, produced these results: "Some 15,000 taxpayers whose returns were audited in 1964 were not audited in 1965 as a result of this innovation." When the step is fully operational, it should eliminate many repetitive audits. But at the same time, the computers will multiply the number of candidates to be audited for other reasons. The only reason why Internal Revenue hasn't audited more returns in the past, as one of IRS's assistant commissioners told the House Appropriation Subcommittee in 1965, has been a lack of manpower to pick out returns. Its Audit Divisions simply cannot recruit and train accountants fast enough.

•

Meanwhile, Internal Revenue does, in effect, use freelance amateur auditors. The situation is a genuine American phenomenon.

5

Free-Lance Auditors:
Tax Tattlers

Public apathy has been dramatically demonstrated by an episode during which 36 adults refused to help or even summon police when a woman was being attacked and killed on a street within their view. Their succinct reasoning: "I didn't want to get involved." Yet, paradoxically, thousands upon thousands of Americans annually volunteer to help the Internal Revenue Service audit income tax returns. Such free-lance investigators, who form an integral part of Internal Revenue's enforcement operations, make their existence known at one small desk at the IRS Manhattan District office. The man who occupies that desk periodically sorts letters into three trays stenciled: Audit, Collection, and Intelligence. However, all letters had, on one particular day, identical themes:

"My former husband has $350 a month put in another

name and doesn't report it on his taxes," the first hand-written note began.

"A man I used to work for makes over $40,000 a year profit but only turns in $11,000 for taxes," said another. "His name is. . . ."

"You should investigate these tax dodgers," a woman wrote. "They're supposed to make $9,000, but they carry big wads of money and spend $40,000 on wild living and everybody knows they cheat and put it in secret Swiss bank accounts."

Each year, Internal Revenue Service's district offices receive an estimated 125,000 letters, telephone calls and personal visits from persons exposing alleged income tax evaders. These tips, called "information items" by IRS employees, are mostly from former spouses and girl friends, disgruntled employees, jealous neighbors and relatives, rumormongers, and profiteers seeking reward money. Tax informers, upon filing *Application and Public Voucher for Reward for Original Information,* Form 211, are paid from 1 to 10 percent of any delinquent taxes collected as a result of their tips. These rewards are paid from Congress' annual unpublicized appropriation of $500,000. But in fiscal 1965, tax-informing became such a growing business that Internal Revenue needed a supplementary allotment. IRS paid $597,731 to 792 informers and rejected another 3,610 claims.

The 3,610 rejected claims for rewards illustrate a disturbing fact: Since informers are unaccountable for any investigation originating from their tip, bounty hunters can consistently make wild guesses. Tipsters may collect part of any unpaid taxes and penalties (average individual reward: $755) if they guess correctly, lose nothing if their lead is erroneous. Hence some informers—particularly a few bookkeepers, accountants, secretaries, bank employees, divorce lawyers, private detectives and policemen who suspect tax improprieties—attempt to make a secondary business from tax rewards.

Such tax profiteers might be equated with that unsavory breed who regard a slight escalator or automobile accident as a business opportunity—to sue. One informer, a New Yorker, furnished some insight into tax tattlers' character when he shed his anonymity in 1964 and angrily wrote then Senator Kenneth Keating of New York that he had not received his reward of about $4,000. The informer, it turned out, had not even paid his own taxes for the previous three years and IRS had applied the reward money against his delinquent bill. The situation is not infrequent. Internal Revenue automatically investigates the return of anyone whom it pays for an "information item" and has found repetitive irony: Paid informers frequently don't declare their reward money on their tax return. In a classic case, a woman who was paid $11,000 for exposing how the owner of a wallpaper company evaded taxes was later fined $5,000 and sentenced to two months in prison for failing to report that reward.

The majority of informers' accusations appear to be motivated by vengeance or jealousy. It is not uncommon today for relatives in bitter arguments to threaten to "turn you in for chiseling on taxes" or warn "tax man'll be coming to see you, buddy." While most hot-tempered threats are valueless unless accompanied by some specific lead, IRS agents admittedly welcome emotional outbursts from angry wives, girl friends and bitter or dismissed employees. "A jilted wife can usually lead right to the evidence," emphasizes one supervisor. Such a case resulted when one tax-evading husband had the effrontery to use the identical surname to simultaneously register his pregnant wife and pregnant mistress at the same hospital. After the wife learned about the incident, she sued for divorce and telephoned Internal Revenue that her husband often failed to report some of his deals transacted in cash. What evidence did she have? "Just look under the back seat of his car," she replied. IRS agents found $10,000 inside the automobile cushion.

Employees who use the tax informant system to "get" their employer or boss often can furnish equally precise documentation of fraud: "He keeps the real tax figures in a loose-leaf scrapbook." Perhaps no such tax informer ever directly led Internal Revenue to more incriminating evidence of tax evasion than the time a dentist's nurse-secretary telephoned IRS's Los Angeles office. The dentist had concealed large amounts of his income, the nurse alleged, and, since he was then on vacation, IRS could inspect his records. When two IRS agents arrived at the office, the nurse, employed by the dentist for 15 years, showed them a card file listing the dentist's actual receipts. The agents copied the records and had such irrefutable evidence of fraud that, when the suntanned dentist returned from vacation, he had no choice but to plead guilty.

Moreover, these insiders expose income schemes that escape the imagination of skilled investigators. In one particularly bizarre incident, an informer told Internal Revenue that an eastern undertaker had not reported the money that he received from secretly selling the gold dental fillings extracted from bodies. Agents found that

85

the mortician had not paid taxes on $6,500 that he received for the gold.

About 90 percent of this category of informers do not apply for reward money, indicating that their motive largely is a grudge rather than greed. Still, one-time employees usually are in such strategic positions within a firm that those who do file formal claims invariably receive the highest rewards. An attorney's secretary, for example, gave Internal Revenue agents her boss' files that proved his tax evasion, then collected $37,500 from the government. And four bookkeepers have held since 1940 the record informers' reward of $79,999.93 for reporting a transport company's president who evaded several million dollars in taxes through fictitious foreign subsidiaries.

As shadowy and un-American as paying brother to spy upon brother appears, Internal Revenue's informer program has compensations. Primarily, informers make would-be tax evaders feel further watched and thereby frighten some of them to report all taxable income. Too, the system traps tax cheaters on all income levels. In 1965 alone, Internal Revenue used paid informers' tips to collect $12.9 million in taxes and developed unpaid informants' leads to gather about $150 million in taxes that it otherwise would not have collected.

Internal Revenue gets these results largely because of a continuing policy. IRS agents, who maintain that their job is to collect taxes and not judge informers, feel only an investigation can determine a tip's authenticity. There is some logic in this position. "Crank letters are not always easy to detect unless you recognize the name," says a supervisor at IRS's Manhattan District office. "I really know one—a housewife has written almost every week for over 10 years exposing the milkmen, movers, missionaries. Just everybody. She always signs her name, so we know right away that the tip is worthless. But if practically the same information comes in an unsigned letter, well, it makes you wonder." Another indication of a crank letter is when it discloses "a million dollar tax evasion" by someone who, say, operates a small newspaper stand. Or the informant might say, as one midwesterner alleged, that ragpickers on a city dump were "evading $2 to $3.50 a day to finance riotous living."

But most tips don't sound this ridiculous and aren't judged to be from cranks. Thus, despite what is said for public consumption, most accusations about tax chiselers are not funneled into Internal Revenue's wastebaskets and incinerators. Every seemingly legitimate tip is evaluated and, to varying degrees, "looked into" or "reviewed." Such phrases are used to avoid the term "investigated." So ponder what can happen if the lady living next door wrote that she saw rolls of $20 bills in your dresser suggesting an illegitimate income. That letter, which would be examined by a supervisor in either Internal Revenue's Collection, Audit or Intelligence Division, would cause, at the least, an audit of your latest return. You might be called in and questioned. Then if a group supervisor in the Audit Division suspected that you concealed income, he would refer the case to Intelligence. That step would likely initiate a review of your past tax returns, bank accounts, employment records, credit ratings, liabilities and purchases. If an agent found that you might have deposited or spent more money than reported on your tax return, he probably would question your acquaintances. If the agent did not find sufficient evidence to warrant a "preliminary" investigation, the Intelligence Division still would open a card file on you. (The card files in the Manhattan District's Intelligence Division stretch almost from wall to wall.) Then if your return is examined or you are suspected of tax evasion in future years, the agent assigned to your case would note the previous allegation that, as one agent puts it, there "was something we couldn't track down."

Consequently, undeserved anxiety sometimes can result from informers' false tips. First, informers and rewards, per se, breed mistrust. Unlike the ancient Greeks and Romans who required the *delator* (common tax informer) to make his accusation in public and stand liable for the same penalties if his charge was wrong, IRS regulations guarantee informers' total anonymity.* The most IRS supervisors say is, "Sons turn in fathers, mothers report daughters, brothers expose brothers and wives report husbands especially if a bitter divorce or quick remarriage by the husband is involved." Hence when anyone is audited or investigated, inquisitive relatives, neighbors and employees can become the No. 1 suspect. As one agent has explained: "Most times you make an unscheduled call on a taxpayer, he usually says, 'I know who sent you.'"

Consider, for example, the situation of a high-living salesman from Chicago who asked three more prosperous relatives at a Christmas party in 1961: "Business up or down this year?" Within a year, the three men—all in

---

* In 1964, U.S. District Court in New York ruled that any informer's identity must be revealed when his information was used as a basis for an arrest or search. The ruling is unlikely to result in the disclosure of tax informers. By the time a person is prosecuted for tax evasion, Internal Revenue has developed evidence—usually records or the lack of payment—that is used in a trial. The informer neither testifies nor is mentioned in court.

separate private businesses and two in different tax districts—were audited or questioned by Internal Revenue. Their returns were found to be honest and only were disallowed minor deductions and assessed additional tax. Next year they were audited again. All three suspect the cousin, an inveterate horseplayer, as being a tax informer. They have no practical means of learning otherwise.

The few taxpayers—and tax evaders—who do learn the identity of tax tattlers often retaliate. Undoubtedly the most persistent was a manufacturer in New England whose former bookkeeper reported him to Internal Revenue in reprisal for being fired. Each time the girl got a new job, the manufacturer told her boss that she was a "paid tax spy" who specialized in "copying books" and "handing them over to the government." Ultimately she was forced to move to another state to keep a job.

Second, it is indeed nerve-racking to pay all taxes that are legally due, then be repeatedly audited as a suspected tax chiseler. Internal Revenue agents, who must look for suspects, have a human habit of staying with someone whom informers report. "Once somebody is reviewed [audited] for any reason [including a tip], they seem to be reviewed practically every year even if they're honest," maintains Senator John Williams of Delaware, a member of Congress's Joint Committee on Internal Revenue Taxation.

Inevitably, tax informers have been denounced, but seldom more vehemently than by T. Coleman Andrews, the Internal Revenue Service's commissioner from 1953–55: * "I would not regard any tax system that makes

* Andrews also campaigned to eliminate the income tax after his term as commissioner of Internal Revenue.

people informers against each other as being compatible with our American concept of government . . . I hold that any tax system is fundamentally unsound that cannot be enforced without encouraging people to be stool pigeons."

Several congressmen, when queried, took contrasting positions about the informer system. One senator said that informers "smack of a totalitarian government where children are encouraged to spy on parents"; while a congressman stressed that informers "assure that everyone pays only his fair share of taxes." If a composite opinion could be made, it would be this: "If I advocate paid informers, that's encouraging police state tactics; if I oppose them, I'd be accused of facilitating tax evasion."

Income tax evasion is, undeniably, an enormous problem. Despite Internal Revenue's threats of harsh punishment for evaders, certain individuals who transact business in cash would never report their genuine income unless their schemes were known to IRS's Intelligence Division. Significantly, some of Intelligence's largest cases originate from informers' tips. Yet most usable tips are only a clue. A special agent must ferret out hidden evidence that establishes beyond doubt there is a deliberate and willful intent to evade taxes.

6

Finding the "Willful" Evaders

The Intelligence Division's 1,750 special agents are assigned to uncover hidden evidence that proves about 1,000 taxpaying Americans annually commit a felony: They deliberately and willfully concealed substantial income, falsified tax returns, or failed to file a return in order to evade federal taxes. Since such deception often is shrewdly masked by unrecorded cash transactions and pseudonyms, it cannot be detected by examining tax returns. Agents must work from leads. Surprisingly, many leads flow in as easily as informers' tips—the clues appear in daily newspapers.

Consequently, several copies of the New York *Daily News* can be seen in the special agents' two long rows of glass-partitioned cubicles on the 20th floor of Internal Revenue's Manhattan District office. Often the tabloid is folded back to page three, which traffics in accounts of muggings and burglaries that involve substantial losses in furs, jewels and cash; messy divorces and lawsuits; and arrests of burglars, abortionists, madams, swindlers and bribe recipients. These incidents bring an automatic response from most inquisitive agents: "Does the couple who lost $25,000 in furs and jewels report an income to afford such luxury?" "Does the old tycoon the young gal is hitting for big alimony report that much income?" "Will the burglar's statement to police mention which homes had lots of cash hidden in safes?" "Doctors don't usually report illegal abortion fees."

Reactions are, in effect, virtually identical in Internal Revenue's other district offices. Agents not only read, but meticulously clip and file comparable items from all daily newspapers, hobby and country club magazines, the *Morning Telegraph (Daily Racing Form)*, neighborhood weeklies and self-service society papers that chronicle such events as someone buying a boat or attending the Kentucky Derby. When a clipping or accumulation of clippings about an individual has attracted an agent's interest, he prints the taxpayer's name on a Revenue Form 2275, asks for his supervisor's signature, and requisitions the fresh suspect's latest return. If that taxpayer has been quoted as saying that he lost $1,500 in cash to muggers on Manhattan's West 89th Street and has listed a taxable income of only $5,000 a year, his problem may have just begun.

Many of Internal Revenue's largest cases have originated in this manner. Go back to March 2, 1952, for example, when most of the nation's daily newspapers printed an Associated Press dispatch from Reno, Nevada. LaVerne Redfield and his wife had driven to a casino to play roulette and left their watchdog in charge of their 15-room, 3-story home. Burglars, meanwhile, had pacified the dog with a piece of ham from Redfield's refrigerator and carried away a 400-pound safe hidden behind clothing in the first-floor, front bedroom closet. The safe, Redfield and Reno's district attorney were quoted as saying, contained nearly $2.5 million in negotiable securities, currency and jewelry. This was not just the largest robbery in American history; it was twice as big as the storied Brinks armored-car robbery in Boston. Redfield also added that he "wasn't about to go on relief." Why, the thieves, he announced, had missed another million dollars' worth of endorsed stock securities that were hidden in an old suitcase.

Investors seldom endorse stock certificates before they sell them, IRS agents sensed, unless the stock is registered in someone else's name. That appeared to be just what had happened. In response to IRS's inquiries, Redfield was reported as unknown in Wall Street financial circles. Another source did vaguely remember him—as an unsuccessful oilman in California during the 1930's. Now Internal Revenue couldn't conceal its interest. Telephone calls to IRS, even to the Commissioner's office, brought an enthusiastic answer: "You're doggone right we're interested!" After an exchange of calls between IRS's National and Reno District offices, an Intelligence supervisor examined Redfield's returns and found that they listed only net amounts for capital gains and dividends, with no supporting schedules to explain the sources.

Now Redfield was put under surveillance. Finally, on May 27, 1960—eight years after the burglary—Redfield was indicted for allegedly failing to report $512,596 in income (tax liability: $256,672) from 1953 through 1956. Government prosecutors used 400 exhibits and 89 wit-

nesses to document its charge that Redfield had maintained 12 brokerage trading accounts in the names of
friends and relatives under the pretense that the profits
were used to finance political campaigns. Redfield, whom
IRS estimated possessed $20 million, didn't even hire a
defense attorney for the trial. Instead he used character
witnesses, including one woman who said he could be
trusted because "he was the best little moneymaker" she
had ever known. Furthermore, the millionaire argued, his
only problem was that he had been too helpful to other
people and that federal taxes were too high. He was
sentenced to five years in prison and fined $10,000.

When Internal Revenue's agents note these large burglaries, their thoughts can travel in two directions. A burglary that causes IRS to investigate the victim does not
mean that agents ignore the burglar's own tax returns
even if he draws a long prison sentence. That's how
Internal Revenue caught Sam Hoover, a criminal defense
attorney and former mayor of Pasadena, Texas. According
to court testimony, Hoover often provided bond without
fee for habitual criminals, then compelled the ex-convicts
to divide what they called the "score" (receipts) from
burglaries committed throughout six states and Mexico.
Once, a criminal testified, Hoover boldly used a telephone
to direct three thieves who were ransacking an elegant
home to torture the wealthy occupant until he revealed
where the "big money" was hidden. On August 5, 1964, a
Texas State jury convicted Hoover of supervising the
torture robbery and, since he was sentenced to 60 years in
prison, he would be expected to drop into indefinite anonymity. But Internal Revenue prudently recognizes all
income—whether it is produced by bank tellers or bank

94

robbers—as taxable income. And Hoover's 1957–60 tax returns, special agents found, didn't include his alleged receipts from the burglaries!

IRS agents interviewed about 300 prison inmates and parolees, many of whom said they had split receipts from burglaries with Hoover. Next agents interviewed approximately 200 of Hoover's legitimate law clients and found evidence that 40 persons had paid him fees (ranging from $60 to $1,500) which also weren't reported as taxable income. The point was not hard to prove. Hoover's own bank deposit tickets also listed the source of each deposit. Thus, on January 21, 1965, Hoover was back in court to face charges of income tax evasion. The bizarre seven-day trial that followed perhaps is best characterized by the reaction of an alternate juror who leaped up and announced: "I've heard enough!" (He was promptly dismissed by the judge.) Hoover was found guilty and received another eight years in prison and a $10,000 fine for failing to report approximately $57,000 in income from law practice and from burglaries and robberies allegedly committed at his direction.

Make no mistake, though, about special agents' investigative techniques. They are human and naturally react to obvious news stories. But agents are not temporarily incapacitated by a newspaper strike or lack of mail from informers. Most agents are aggressively prying. They take the offensive and ferret out clues. "How are some ways we get our leads?" mused Andrew Hankowski, a veteran agent and intelligence analyst in IRS's National Office. He lit a paper match and let it burn slowly as he answered the question in a barely audible voice. "Oh, by being a little like the real life spy business. Incredibly dull. You look and listen for general conversations, third-party conversations, rumors about underhand deals, indiscriminate speech. You look and listen."

Special agents, to be sure, look and listen in particular places. They frequently obtain identities of purchasers of large homes or safes, check registrations of yachts and small private planes, first-class passenger lists on luxury liners, and country club memberships. They appear, always inconspicuously, at fashionable auction houses (such as New York's Parke-Bernet Galleries) where business often is transacted in cash, not checks, and initials, not names. They observe large wedding receptions and debutante balls for multiple reasons: to determine if the father's reported income enables him to afford such expenditures and, even so, has he diverted tax-deductible business expenses, such as liquor, to pay for the private party? As one former commissioner of IRS has theorized, "It's pretty hard—no more than a 50–50 chance—for anyone to have lavish blowouts or spend freely except out of capital or find some way to get it out of their taxes." In a type of case that occurs frequently an agent found that a novelty manufacturer deducted his daughter's wedding reception expenses of $6,245.97 from his taxes for "travel, entertainment and shop expenses" because he included 90 customers among the 320 guests. (IRS disallowed the deduction.)

Sometimes agents take the automobile license numbers of pretentious guests. Once, in leaving a party in Washington, D.C., a special agent from IRS's Maryland District was passed by a horn-blowing driver who epitomized the *nouveau riche*. He wore a garish green suit and brandished a long cigar between his second and third fingers.

The woman wore a full-length chinchilla. Neither appeared refined. Alertly, the agent copied the license number and later found that the automobile's owner reported an annual income of about $5,000. After a long investigation, IRS agents revealed that the horn-blower's actual income ranged between $25,000 and $35,000 and he owed $85,000 in back taxes and interest.

The vast majority of leads distilled from someone enjoying his wealth or being thrust into public attention, do not, of course, result in the detection of master tax evaders. Neither do most genuinely wealthy individuals, whose lawyers often can find sufficient legal loopholes to avoid taxes, foolishly attempt tax evasion. Yet most knowledgeable millionaires know that publicity can bring additional scrutiny from IRS agents. Hence many of today's millionaires live in semi-anonymity, unlike the 19th century millionaires such as John D. Rockefeller and Edward H. Harriman, who became rich before the Age of Internal Revenue and promoted their wealth into fame. One vivid illustration is John D. MacArthur, an outspoken, mustached man of 70, who has made an estimated $300 million from 12 insurance companies since World War II. He lives in such a simple bungalow in a subdivision (which he owns) outside West Palm Beach, Florida, that it puzzles first-time visitors. There are no expensive paintings, no Kirman rugs, no antiques that usually attract a layout in the *New York Times* society section or *Town and Country* magazine.* Such attention, MacArthur has told an interviewer, makes a man vulnerable to two money-minded individuals who use binoculars: kid-

* MacArthur is by no means a miser. He paid the $25,000 needed to ransom the DeLong Ruby that had been stolen from New York's Museum of Natural History.

nappers and agents from what he has called that "nosing around *Infernal* Internal Revenue Service."

Internal Revenue Service's agents, though, have techniques to observe dealings of the quiet ones. It is largely a game of waiting and watching. Agents, for one thing, watch for activity of persons on IRS's master list—an alphabetical index of subjects that ranges from grand dragons (of the Klu Klux Klan) to gregarious waiters. Consider, for instance, the morning that a special agent in New York scanned a Wall Street brokerage firm's list of new investors. When the agent saw that a Hans Paul had invested over $10,000, he knew that Internal Revenue now had a tangible lead. The Intelligence Division hadn't forgotten that Hans Paul, ostensibly just another retired man living in Florida, had been better known for nine years as "Mr. Hans," the dignified headwaiter at New York's Waldorf-Astoria Hotel banquet division. As often occurs, headwaiters' tax returns do not include all the folded currency that diners ease into their hands to get a good table or make an impression.* After IRS agents investigated for two years, a Federal Grand Jury indictment charged that Hans had reported only $55,605 of his $122,677 income (salary: $10,900; tips: $111,777) over a four-year period. Paul pleaded guilty to one count, evading $8,682 in one year, and was sentenced to four months in prison and fined $7,500.

Moreover, even money, per se, is considered a lead. Anytime some unexplained currency turns up, Internal Revenue agents can assume that it is nonreported taxable income unless the owner can prove otherwise. This theory

---

* In 1965, the U.S. Tax Court ruled IRS can estimate the income of waiters who didn't keep records of their tips.

has been responsible for countless investigations—and subsequent convictions—of tax evaders. And the position has become rather inflexible. Take the time when Internal Revenue's Philadelphia District office received the Federal Reserve System's Form CR-1—which is used to note any large or unusual currency transactions—reporting that a couple had attempted to exchange $45,000 in moldy currency that appeared to have been buried. Internal Revenue took all of the $45,000 (and then some) in back taxes and penalties because the couple could not prove how they accumulated such a sum nor had they included it in their reported income.

Regardless of who competes for large amounts of disputed currency, IRS always seems to win. Perhaps no such incident surpasses what has become known as the case of Moriarty's Millions. The episode began in 1962 when Joseph (Newsboy) Moriarty, one-time bookmaker and gambling racket leader in Jersey City, New Jersey, was sent to Trenton State Prison on a conviction for gambling tax violations. Shortly afterwards, on July 3, 1962, two members of a demolition crew working in Moriarty's Oxford Street neighborhood entered a garage and found an abandoned 1947 automobile trunk stuffed with $10, $20, $50 and $100 bills. Excitedly, the men called the FBI. The FBI agents needed until midnight to count the money—$2,438,110. Now apparently aware that papers in the trunk could connect the money to him, Moriarty filed an amended income tax return listing income for that year as $2.4 million. He also filed a claim for his money, as did the two workmen, the garage owner, the Jersey City, Hudson County and New Jersey State governments, and Internal Revenue. Although IRS had a tax

INSIDE INTERNAL REVENUE

lien of only $335,000 against Moriarty, it quickly added
another lien of $3,395,665.53, then raised the bill to $11
million. It was no contest. The court awarded all of
Moriarty's money to IRS in July of 1965.

Who are the men who do this work and have authority
to arrest and recommend prosecution? Each IRS District
Office has an Intelligence Division staffed by special
agents who are responsible for detecting local tax law
violators. But since new agents are specially trained and
some investigations may require coordinating several districts (and sometimes regions), much of the Intelligence
Division's work also revolves around Internal Revenue's
headquarters in Washington, D.C. The hub is a series of
large, bright rooms on the seventh floor of the National
Office building where veteran officers are frequently on
the telephone, centered around a conference table, and
sending women to pull out files. The person plainly in
command—the director of the Intelligence Division—is
William A. Kolar, a stern-looking but friendly man.*
Stocky, black-haired and red-faced and often dressed in a
blue suit and pin-stripe shirt, Kolar has been an investigator (for the Senate Judiciary Committee, FBI and Internal Revenue) for 22 of his 48 years. The assistant
director, Robert Manzi, is a short, direct, calm man with
20 years' experience in IRS's Intelligence Division. In
many ways, Manzi's calmness typifies how IRS's special
agents are ideally supposed to appear: cold, unemotional
gatherers of evidence.

Today, special agents are trained for this purpose

* Kolar was appointed to the position on December 20, 1965, suc-
ceeding H. Alan Long, who became director of IRS's Pittsburgh
District Office. Many cases mentioned in this chapter occurred while
Long headed the Intelligence Division.

100

rather than promoted from within Internal Revenue. Each year IRS recruits about 125 prospective agents, who must either pass an investigative aptitude test, have four years of college, including 12 hours of accounting, or graduate study in business, police administration or criminology. Then the trainees undergo nearly a year's internship, which begins with a five-week course in basic tax law. Next the men receive seven-weeks training at the Treasury Law Enforcement Training School in downtown Washington, D.C. These prospective agents, along with Secret Service and Bureau of Narcotics trainees, are taught conventional detection skills: surveillance; how to search for concealed evidence; read scribbled notes or coded punch cards; photograph documents or contents of wastebaskets; take fingerprints and plaster casts; learn judo and the operation of firearms, tape recorders and microphones; how to interrogate persons who will be reticent or openly hostile; avoid planted traps (*i.e.,* interviewing a woman alone), arrest, write reports and testify in court.

Ultimately, trainees face simulated cases in which they must find 82 percent of the concealed evidence to pass the course. If they pass—and nearly all do—they become appointees and spend at least six months working from a district office with an experienced special agent. Then the appointee is designated a special agent and issued a badge, handcuffs and .38 caliber revolver with choice of a two- or four-inch barrel. Most take the handier two-inch barrel. At this point, the majority of new special agents end their formal training. But new agents who do not fully develop, in the judgment of their supervisor, often return to Washington in three or four years for refresher courses.

Furthermore, about 30 first-class agents needed for specialized work are selected to return each year to the same building to attend an "Advanced Technical Investigative Aid School" that was secretly begun in 1955. The school's purpose had been, until 1965, to teach agents how to work undercover and use, among other things, such crafts as planting telephone wiretaps and secret listening devices; how to operate tieclasp and wristwatch radios, obtain combinations to safe locks, and how to pick locks on doors within three minutes. Special Agent James J. O'Neill told a Senate subcommittee in 1965 that he had graduated from the school with complete familiarity of "burglar tools." Later Agent O'Neill was even proven to be an accomplished lock-picker. How was this fact known? "He has picked some locks in our office when we have forgotten our keys," said George Wilson, an IRS group supervisor.

Specialized skills, what few times they can be used, are only a supplementary weapon. The skill that special agents learn—or develop themselves—is to collect evidence, not excuses that it can't be done. Some special agents' techniques are ingeniously original: Years ago in trying to affix the income of a whorehouse in Atlantic City, New Jersey, undercover agents personally verified that each job cost $10 and that each customer received a clean white towel. Then an agent obtained the linen service's records, multiplied by 10 the number of towels the bawdyhouse received, and established gross taxable income, which was upheld in court. Elsewhere, IRS agents have hidden in a cave to observe the number of customers entering and leaving a suspected tax evader's business; have paid private garbage collectors to give them refuse from a suspect's wastebasket; and visited doctors' offices as "patients," familiarized themselves with the doctor's schedule and office layout, then sent an "accountant" (another undercover agent) to trick a part-time receptionist into giving him the doctor's personal records. Such artifices give Internal Revenue agents a tactical advantage. Sometimes, attorney's associations contend, agents have incriminating evidence on suspected tax evaders before the individuals realize that they are in serious trouble with Internal Revenue.

Comfortingly, special agents' cloak-and-dagger tactics are seldom used on the so-called average taxpayer who misconstrues a tax law. When the Intelligence Division detects someone who is guilty of negligent errors, misinterpretations, questionable deductions (unless entirely fictionalized), apparent underpayment and late returns, the case usually is referred to IRS's Audit or Collection divisions. In such instances, the taxpayer may be summoned to court as an administrative action for civil fraud, a misdemeanor which can result in a fine of 50 percent of any unpaid tax.

The Intelligence Division's special agents pursue only cases of suspected flagrant tax violations which can result in prosecution for a felony. This charge often is one of the most difficult to prove. Evidence that a man evaded taxes is not enough for criminal prosecution. Intelligence's agents must substantiate that the violator's motive was both willful and deliberate or, as William Kolar puts it, "We almost have to prove state of mind." In doing this work in 1965, Internal Revenue's agents examined an

103

estimated 150,000 leads, tips and unverified rumors that resulted in, according to IRS statistics, 8,786 preliminary investigations and 3,643 full-scale investigations. Then Internal Revenue recommended to the Justice Department that 1,005 individuals be prosecuted on criminal charges involving $122.2 million in taxes and interest. Subsequently there were 823 indictments, with 572 persons pleading guilty or *nolo contendere,* 73 others convicted by trial, 50 acquitted and the remaining cases dismissed or never brought to trial.*

The tax evaders were, as usual, a diverse collection that included at least one mayor, city councilman, state legislator, judge, "civic leader," "prominent" lawyer, doctor, dean, manufacturer, merchant, accountant, publisher, author, actor, banjo player, broker, bookie, gravedigger, contractor, and union boss.

Although their backgrounds differ, convicted tax evaders have a common trait: They show no intention of paying their legal tax. Look at the intricate scheme of The Towel Tycoon. Internal Revenue's Philadelphia District office became interested in Morris Goldberg, a large linen supplier, when a federal judge fined him and two of his corporations $55,000 and placed him on probation after a plea of no defense to the Justice Department's charge of attempting to monopolize the linen rental service through price-fixing, manipulated bids to public agents and harassing competitors. Men who rig bids, Internal Revenue has found, frequently rig income taxes. But when revenue agents analyzed Goldberg's corporation tax returns, they found an incredibly entangled accounting system that

* The average sentence for income tax evasion is 13.1 months. The average time served is 7.8 months.

appeared to defy any auditor. The linen business was spread over 13 separate corporations, some operating on a fiscal year basis, others on a calendar year. Thousands and thousands of dollars—particularly the steady loans which the corporations received and punctually repaid—were shuffled from corporation to corporation.

In an effort to penetrate the barrier, special agents obtained thousands of microfilmed bank deposit slips and checks and painstakingly recreated Goldberg's transactions. They traced each entry, even finding checks that had been cashed at racetracks and gambling establishments. Finally, after three years, Internal Revenue had constructed a case. According to an indictment, Goldberg and an administrative assistant had disguised his gross receipts by listing many sales as "loans," then doubled the understatement of net profits by using genuine funds to repay the mythical loans. Six hundred and thirty-nine exhibits, representing 4,000 pieces of paper, were needed just to outline the scheme, which, of course, was not willingly clarified by Goldberg. He initially "misplaced" his records, but, when subpoenaed, had some books brought in musty clothes hampers to the U.S. District Courthouse. After a five-week trial, a federal jury found Goldberg guilty of an eight-count conspiracy to evade $885,000 in income taxes.

A more numerous but less sophisticated breed of arithmetic artists obtain their entire income by challenging Internal Revenue's special agents. Calling themselves "tax consultants," "accountants," "tax savers," "experts," or "tax practitioners," they flourish by guaranteeing income tax refunds for their clients. Such phony consultants create mythical dependents or illegal deductions, take their share of the "refund" in advance ("we usually split 50–50"), then transform the impressed taxpayer into a tax evader by inducing him to sign a false return. By the time IRS's special agents have caught the taxpayer, the "consultant" is in another town, usually under a different alias and different colored wig or toupee. Internal Revenue does set standards for tax practitioners: Only the 80,000 persons who hold Treasury Department Practitioners' Cards—attorneys, certified public accountants or former Internal Revenue employees and persons who have passed a written examination—can represent taxpayers before the IRS. Furthermore, Internal Revenue's Director of Practice annually reviews about 250 derogatory complaints against such approved tax practitioners and sometimes invalidates a card.

Nonetheless, any con man with a sign, pencil and some blank 1040 returns can prepare tax returns for a fee. Such "experts," along with an army of reasonably honest but often incompetent tax-return preparers, emerge each February in small offices, cubbyholes, drugstores, barbershops, bars, delicatessens, and churches. A church was, for example, the base for the "Believe-It-Or-Not" tax consultant. This tax expert had been featured in Ripley's "Believe It or Not" series back in 1937 because he had lost both arms in a boyhood railroad accident but could write, type and remain entirely self-sufficient with artificial limbs and hooks. Because of the tax expert's handicap, sympathetic pastors allowed him to solicit clients in Chicago churches until, as Federal Judge Richard B. Austin later said, he had convinced many people that he "was Lord of the green pastures on 58th Street." In 1955, the expert foresaw such a large business that he incorporated a nonprofit organization in Chicago to prepare its members' tax returns and furnish legal advice.

Usually the Expert began his spiel with a baited question: Of course, you received a large tax refund last year? When anyone said, "no," the Expert angrily castigated Internal Revenue for forcing the person to file a short Form 1040A when an itemized Form 1040 allowed greater deductions. He, the Expert, would obtain refunds for all members of his organization. The prospective client filled out an application and was formally accepted by the Expert's organization. When the Expert filled out the new client's tax return, witnesses testified, he often convinced single men that they were married to their girl friends, that divorcées still were married, and that married couples had two or three fictitious children. Typical interviewing, according to testimony, went like this:

Tax Expert: "Are you married?" (and thus receiving a $600 tax exemption).

Client: "No."

Tax Expert: "Yes you are!"

Always the Expert had each applicant sign a blank 1040 return and two "depositions" that listed all exemptions and deductions plus, unbeknown to the taxpayers, a power of attorney authorizing him to cash their refund check. Then he listed even more fictitious dependents on the presigned tax return, claimed a large refund, used the foundation's address and obliterated the taxpayer's address on his Form W-2. The client received the "carbon" which showed his correct address and a refund claim usually about $200 to $300 less than what had been claimed. Most of the refunds were paid. When refunds were later challenged and IRS special agents were sent to track down the recipients, the Expert had already warned the individuals to expect someone from Internal Revenue but to refer him to their "tax advisor." Finally, when many taxpayers didn't receive any refund, they complained to Internal Revenue. After a long investigation of bank records special agents found that the Expert's organization had deposited over $40,000 in refund checks during 1960–61 alone. Brought into federal court in November of 1963, on charges of preparing false tax returns, the Expert astonished the jury by constantly flipping page after page of documents with his hooks and tongue. Still the jury deliberated only one hour and 15 minutes before finding him guilty. He was sentenced to two years in prison.

A second breed of specialized tax evaders are the "Ten Percenters," who appeared at horse-race tracks the day after IRS issued a regulation in 1960: Anyone who cashes a ticket for more than $600 for a $2 bet or $3,000 on a $10 wager must furnish identification, Social Security number, sign IRS Form 1090 and declare such winnings as taxable income. Thus a man in the 35 percent income tax bracket realized that a ticket worth $1,000 would net him only $650 after taxes and often responded to a Ten Percenter's tempting offer: "I'll cash the ticket and use my identification for only 10 percent. You'll make $250 more."

Ten Percenters became big business in late 1963 when the twin double, a new long-shot craze, was added at many tracks. Twin-double bets, which entail attempting to pick consecutive winners of the sixth through ninth races, resulted in individual $2 payoffs of $129,631, $132,322 and $171,084 just at New York's two harness-racing tracks, Yonkers and Roosevelt raceways. Since 85 percent of the amount bet in the twin-double pool is divided among ticketholders who pick the most winners, a dozen or so persons win at least $2,000 and up every night. Accordingly, there also were, by 1965, organized syndicates with counterfeit Social Security cards and runners who circulated among crowds asking, "Who's got a live one?" The runners attempted to buy the tickets or cash them for a fee.

One 12-member syndicate, according to a federal indictment, grew so large that it cashed tickets valued at $10 million and cheated the government out of $1.5 million in taxes in a single year. It became discernible one Friday night at one of Yonkers Raceway's standup bars that active recruiting was one reason why the syndicate continued to increase its volume. When a syndicate member met an alert horseplayer, they often hired him. Thus they couldn't miss a short, medium-built horseplayer with binoculars slung around his neck, when he rushed to the bar wearing a winner's facial expression. "Double bourbon on the rocks," said the horseplayer, who shall be called Al Gordon. He fished a ticket from his shirt pocket, then smiled and put the ticket back in his pocket. "You've got a live one," volunteered a man who said his name was Carl. "And you don't look dumb enough to cash and declare yourself."

Al wasn't that dumb. He sold his ticket to Carl. Two nights later, Al ran into Carl at the bar. He didn't have any winning tickets, but did point out a thin, wavy-haired man. "He's alive," Al said. After Carl bought the wavy-haired man's ticket, he returned to invite Al to dinner that evening and to meet some of the syndicate's bosses. One boss was so impressed with Al's ability to spot twin-double winners that he hired him as a steerer. Al worked for the syndicate for four months, or long enough to identify and photograph the syndicate members with a camera concealed inside his binoculars. "Al Gordon," you see, was one of Internal Revenue's undercover agents. Subsequently on another Friday night Internal Revenue hit. Thirty agents—almost as many agents as horseplayers who held tickets on Yonkers' winning combinations—simultaneously arrested the syndicate's 12 members and led them in handcuffs to the U.S. Marshal's wagon that was parked outside the track.

Not everyone who deliberately and willfully violates a tax law is, of course, led away in handcuffs. Neither does every full-scale investigation of a suspect result in catching a tax evader. Nor do all cases of strongly suspected tax-law violations receive comparable investigations. Since it is illegal for Internal Revenue's personnel to reveal anyone's tax status unless there is reason for the return to become a public record, the full measure of who *is*, and who *is not*, investigated, will never be known. But, as one demonstration of how investigations can contrast, consider the outcome of two cases that occurred during the same 1962–64 period and became public records.

The first example involves a Herbert K. May, who held the politically appointed job of Deputy Assistant Secretary of State for Inter-American Affairs. According to a letter signed by Mortimer Caplin, then IRS Commissioner, May belatedly filed his 1949 tax return in 1951, his 1950 return in 1952 and his 1951 and 1952 returns both in 1953. As a tax delinquent, May, therefore, would theoretically fall into what Internal Revenue personnel call the annual "audit stream" or "examination program" and be caught if he did not file a return. But notice what was found to have transpired between May and Internal Revenue Service from 1953 to 1963, and revealed on October 29, 1963, when Senator John Williams of Delaware rose in the Senate, cleared his throat and began speaking:

I wish to call attention to another situation wherein this Administration, after finding a glaring violation of the law by one of its Frontiersmen, allowed this individual merely to submit a quiet resignation and then promptly proceed to brush the whole episode under the rug. On August 14, 1963, Mr. Herbert K. May had been permitted an "honorable resignation" from the State Department despite eight years of income tax delinquencies.

The record shows that Mr. May not only had a historical record of delinquencies in the filing of his tax returns but also had neglected to file any returns at all during the eight-year period, 1953 to 1961. When this was discovered the only action taken was to allow him in 1963 to file returns retroactively for those delinquent years, 1953 through 1961, and then submit what as far as the public was concerned was an honorable resignation. This is quite a contrast to what would have happened had this been an ordinary laborer or farmer without proper political connections.

Indeed there was a contrast. Willful failure to file an income tax return has sent hundreds of men to prison. However, in view of May's "voluntary disclosure," Internal Revenue said in a statement, ". . . it was the decision of the Service that the prosecutive potential of the case did not warrant referral to the Department of Justice." Internal Revenue's statement did not say why it had not detected that May hadn't filed a return in nearly a decade nor what motivated him to make such a sudden voluntary disclosure.

A full-scale investigation in the second case, meanwhile, was in progress in Massachusetts without such comparable evidence of a violation of tax laws. It had begun three weeks after Special Agent George Wilson, a veteran group supervisor in IRS Intelligence Division, transferred from Chicago to Boston. On January 25, 1962, Wilson called in John B. Flattery, a veteran special agent, and showed him the tax returns filed by Bernard Mc-Garry, who ran a liquor store and tavern in suburban Milton, Massachusetts. While McGarry had no previous conviction for income tax evasion, Wilson said that Mc-Garry was suspected of underreporting his taxable income. The case, he said, had been sent up from Washington and therefore he had classified it as a "big one." Flattery was named case supervisor and, as in other big cases, would utilize several special agents: Robert M. Ferrick, John Noonan, John Crowe, and Jack Harris, the undercover man.

The case received such priority that agents decided to maintain daily surveillance on McGarry's home at 790 Canton Avenue. Accordingly, an agent persuaded one of McGarry's neighbors to allow Internal Revenue to set up a lookout post in a barn loft that provided an unobstructed view of McGarry's driveway. Then, almost every day for the next six months, at least two agents would leave Boston between 4 and 4:30 P.M. to beat the 5 o'clock traffic rush to Milton, and begin their vigil on who entered and left McGarry's house. The first two nights, the agents used a bazooka-like sniperscope, a World War II instrument that Wilson had borrowed from the Coast Guard in Boston. The sniperscope was supposed to enable the agents to read automobile license plates, but they were unable to operate it. After the agents learned how to operate the sniperscope, they found it unsuitable for their needs. "We could not identify anything except a light, a haze and images," Flattery later testified before a Senate subcommittee. "The purpose of reading license plate numbers—it was just out of the question. We could not read them."

After returning the sniperscope, the agents used conventional surveillance techniques. The agent stationed in the loft watched the home through high-powered binoculars, and each time someone opened a door and walked to an automobile, IRS's lookout man would radio another team of agents parked about 50 yards away in a black government automobile. The agents would then cruise past McGarry's home, drop behind the departing vehicle, and record the automobile's license number. Nothing appeared to move from McGarry's driveway without Internal Revenue's knowledge. Even the smallest, most minute detail was noted, as reflected by a page in Flattery's official IRS diary on the night that he followed McGarry to a mailbox. The handwritten page reads:

11–10–62 JBF

10:45 P.M. At O.P.

(Pontiac 1962—Mass Reg #4652) tailed by Longhorn 4 (in front of suspect) and Longhorn 2.

"Took #4652 to Mattepan Square—Car driven by Bernie, who pulled up at mailbox at corner of Blue Hill Ave. & Cummings Highway. He got out carrying large manila envelope. & dropped in mailbox. & then proceeded back to 730 Canton Ave. Instructed Longhorn 4 to take him back home.

S/A Ferrick & I checked the line on the mailbox as to when the next pick-up will be (4:00 P.M. Sunday).

I had a letter to mail, so when I pulled the large slot in

the mailbox the envelope placed there by McGarry had not dropped down & was visible to read. I read the address & to whom it was addressed. It was addressed to

Bernard McGarry Jr.
4300 Spruce St.
Philadelphia 4, Pa.
    (son @ school—Warton School of Finance.)

Simultaneously other agents developed the case during daylight hours. Agents used the license plate numbers to determine the owners of automobiles leaving McGarry's house, then investigated and questioned those persons about any association with McGarry. Agents went to Boston's First National Bank, wrote some names on a pad of IRS forms, and requisitioned the checking account records of McGarry and approximately 300 persons suspected of having visited or done business with McGarry. Then, in an effort to determine McGarry's gross expenditures, agents investigated any place McGarry may have spent money: laundries, garages, groceries, beauty parlors, insurance companies; Philadelphia's Wharton School of Finance, where his son attended school; and a business that installed a lawn sprinkler for McGarry. The Audit Division even pulled and examined the past tax returns of Attorney Lawrence O'Donnell, who was later to defend McGarry and to whom, IRS agents said, McGarry might have paid fees for legal services. Still, after a *year's* intense investigation, Internal Revenue had not proved that McGarry underreported his taxable income.

But, as the agents later testified, a startling discovery had led them to what appeared to have been the "evidence." When an official at Linwood Fabrics Company was questioned on how much the firm was paid to deco-

rate McGarry's home, Special Agent Jack Harris said, he
found the firm's files contained photographs and a floor
plan of McGarry's home. Dutifully getting photocopies of
the floor plan and pictures, Harris took the information to
the Intelligence Division office. There agents reasoned
from the layout that McGarry kept a large safe in his
basement. That safe, at least three (and perhaps all) of
the agents concluded, was probably where the unreported
currency was hidden.

Now how could Internal Revenue look inside the vault?
It was, of course, illegal to enter the house secretly. The
agents couldn't obtain a legal warrant to search someone's
home on suspicion it contained money. Yet they couldn't
substantiate the case unless they knew how much money
was inside the vault.

What did happen? Did Internal Revenue agents break
into the home? Disturbing but repudiated answers
emerged as the McGarry investigation, which now had
extended into its second year, took a strange twist. Harris,
meanwhile, had been indicted in Boston's U.S. District
Court for allegedly accepting a $1,500 bribe. Contending
that he had been framed by Internal Revenue, Harris
went in 1965 before the Senate subcommittee that was
investigating government agencies' invasion of privacy
and testified that he and another agent had sneaked up
against the house for a close look at McGarry's vault:

Yes, sir, I know of another agent, John Noonan, who used
to brag about going up to the lawn and peeking in the windows.
At the local Milton Elks Lodge, he did quite a bit of bragging
about Mr. McGarry, that he was a gangster and he intended
to get him. What he didn't know was that Mr. McGarry's
physician was present and the story went back to McGarry. I,

myself have gone on the premises of the McGarry home. I
have looked in the window. I have crept up along the bushes
beside the house.

Ultimately, Harris further testified, came the chance to
inspect the vault:

When we had arrived this [day]—it must have been late
spring or early summer, because there was still sun out.
Mrs. McGarry was sunning herself. We observed her through
the binoculars . . . She went into the house and I thought
nothing until I got a message from Mr. Crowe saying, "Do you
know she has left the house?"

Asked by the subcommittee's chief counsel, Bernard
Fensterwald, Jr., how he entered the house, Harris replied:

There was a patio in the back of the house with a screen
door. There was another door within the screen door, but
that door was ajar. Apparently when she left the house, she
didn't bother locking up. I thought later she probably went
up to her sister-in-law's house, who lives in the neighborhood . . . I didn't even think of the legalities at the time. I
wasn't sure of what was legal and what wasn't. I just went
in on his [Robert Ferrick's] instruction that now would be a
good time to find out what was in that vault. I was in the
house approximately 6 or 7 minutes. I was quite nervous in
there and I got out.

Nevertheless, Harris continued, the six or seven minutes
that he claimed to have spent inside McGarry's basement
enabled him to make a discovery that exceeded all expec-
tations—the "vault" turned out to be a cedar clothes
closet that had a regular handle and contained clothing
and furs instead of money. Still, the former special agent
added, he copied the name "Leighton Clothing" from the

label inside a sport coat and "Murray Furs" from a fur coat's label.

Special Agent John B. Flattery followed Harris's testimony before the subcommittee by stating that he had no knowledge "whatsoever" nor had he instructed his agents to enter McGarry's house. Agent Robert Ferrick added, when asked about Harris's statement that he entered the house on his instructions, testified: "I believe Mr. Harris was lying about that, sir." Although the IRS agents admitted that Harris had been sent to question the proprietors of Leighton Clothing in New York about McGarry's purchases, they could not explain how Harris could have otherwise obtained the information.

Since testimony describing the alleged illegal entry sharply contradicted, Fensterwald suggested that Agent John J. Crowe (whom Harris said was his lookout during the alleged entry) be summoned as the subcommittee's final witness. Then Robert Spatz, Internal Revenue's lawyer, was asked to telephone Crowe in Boston and arrange his appearance—with the stipulation that Crowe neither discuss nor rehearse his version of the McGarry incident with other IRS personnel. But one of either of two events occurred: Either Crowe was flown to Washington under armed guard, as the subcommittee investigators insist, or he was involved in a remarkable coincidence. Fifteen minutes after Crowe was telephoned from Washington, William Sheehan, a group supervisor in Boston's Intelligence Division, had appeared at Crowe's house to "bring a travel voucher," drive him to the airport, where they waited together for two hours and met two other Internal Revenue employees, Harold L. Smith, assistant chief, Enforcement Division, and Special Agent John Hanley.

Hanley, it turned out, had to take the same 9:15 P.M. flight with Crowe to Washington to deliver what he said were "certain papers and memorandums" and, since he understood there might be "room difficulties," would share a room with Crowe in the Washington Hotel in Washington, D.C. Hanley, whom Senate investigators said carried a pistol, remained with Crowe all night, then took him to the old Senate Office Building the next morning; and when Crowe moved toward investigators, he stepped in and blocked him. Crowe testified that he had participated in the surveillance of McGarry's home, had seen the floor plan and discussed the "safe" in McGarry's basement. But, he added, "I have no knowledge that he [Harris] broke into the premises."

A few minutes later, Bernard Fensterwald, Jr., the subcommittee's counsel, asked a question that obviously stunned Crowe: "Would it be fair to say you are under house arrest with Mr. Hanley?" Crowe, after a slight pause, replied: "I should hope not." That ended Crowe's testimony. Alertly, Fensterwald felt that Crowe, his face puffed and his eyes bloodshot, was obviously ill. He dismissed Crowe as a witness. Fensterwald's assumption was correct. Crowe died of a heart attack a month later.

The anomalous case was perhaps best summarized in two statements by Senator Edward Long of Missouri, the subcommittee chairman. First, he asked Agent Hanley, "Why did not Mr. Crowe bring them [the papers]? He is an agent in your department and was coming here." Then Senator Long asked Flattery, "Does it not seem to you then that there was a great waste of manpower and taxpayers' money in this type of investigation?"

"This was the initiation of the investigation," Flattery

replied, "and the conduct of the investigation was to determine what the tax liability should have been." In plainer language, the facts are that, after investigating McGarry for three years, Internal Revenue's Boston office apparently had no evidence against him. McGarry was never tried for an income tax violation. Likewise neither evidence of deliberate tax evasion nor a trial results in two-thirds of Intelligence's full-scale investigations. But as is recognized by any investigator—whether employed by a Congressional subcommittee or Internal Revenue Service—one must investigate before he has evidence to prove anything.

•

If IRS's Boston District office had, as it was implied before the subcommittee, been assigned the untidy case by the North Atlantic Regional or the National office, then its special agents were only following orders. Systematic decisions are now made by high government officials on whom they want Internal Revenue's Intelligence Divisions to pursue. Already the results—which make the Internal Revenue Service the most forcible government agency ever to oppose organized criminals—have unnerved some of the Mafia's toughest overlords.

7

The Automatic Investigation

He was immaculately dressed—and in many ways a distinguished-looking "businessman"—this Francesco Saveria. But he had an alias (Frank Costello), an FBI number (936217), an underworld code (C. Frank), and three not inappropriate titles (King of the Slots, Prime Minister of the Underworld, and Chairman of the Board of Murder, Inc.). Costello had all of these things because, above all, he was one of the shrewdest of all hoodlums. As he eased into semiretirement at 54, the only crime ever proved that he committed was carrying a pistol without a permit when he was 17 years old. Furthermore, as insulation against the Internal Revenue Service, he took his "cut" in cash, paid for everything in cash and maintained no records. The few documents bearing Frank Costello's name were income tax returns that purported he had an average annual income of $39,000 (from slot machines and a gambling casino in Louisiana) and that he made charitable donations to the National Jewish Hospital,

120

Christopher Columbus Catholic Service and Negro Actors League. No one would ever prove that he was paid a cent more.

But, suddenly, Costello found himself sitting beside a lawyer in U.S. District Court and in big trouble. For two years, three special agents from Internal Revenue's New York Intelligence Division had reconstructed Costello's expenditures dollar by dollar. They determined how much money he had spent for real estate, an apartment on New York's Central Park West, a girl friend's apartment on Fifth Avenue, a home at Sands Point, Long Island, and a chauffeured Cadillac that took him almost daily to the Waldorf-Astoria Hotel; how much he, "C. Frank," his wife Loretta, and intermediaries spent for barbers, manicurists, hairdressers, food, clothing, jewelry, vacations, tips and even flowers, tombstones and a cemetery plot. Fitted together, these small facts gave IRS what is called a net expenditure case. Now all Costello could do was fidget on a shellacked chair in court as 144 witnesses—backed by over 368 exhibits—proved that the Costellos had spent or controlled $140,000 more than his reported income over a four-year period. The mobster was convicted of evading $73,437 in income taxes and, after exhausting appeals in 1958, served 3 1/2 years at Lewisburg Penitentiary, where he could reflect upon his advice to other hoodlums: "Pay your damn taxes, boys. Pay more than you owe!"

Today, more and more organized criminals are paying income taxes, but, like Costello, it provides little immunity from Internal Revenue. IRS does not investigate a hoodlum's return because a peculiarity is noticed. Its District Intelligence Divisions assign specialists to investigate automatically the returns filed by many of the reputed 2,200 syndicated criminals—the ruthless men who are called the Mafia, Cosa Nostra, Brooklyn Gambino Mob, Chicago Syndicate, and the Underworld and whose *soldiers, buttonmen, dons* and *fronts* run multimillion dollar industries in narcotics, loan-sharking, extortion, murder, gambling, prostitution, and planned bankruptcies, then channel some profits into legitimate businesses. Only fractions of this income is, of course, reported on income tax returns and, even so, as derived from fictitious jobs such as "meat salesman."

While Internal Revenue has continually investigated leading mobsters since it caused the imprisonment of Al Capone, the Prohibition era's No. 1 hoodlum, IRS recently intensified the campaign against individuals suspected of having underworld affiliations. The Intelligence Division has done this, not by adding more special agents, but by retraining a few experienced investigators. Some men are taught to work as undercover agents—severing all identity or contact with Internal Revenue, angling into card games with Mafia underlings, taking a menial job in a syndicate-owned business, and possibly detecting about how much money is made. The results, from a numerical viewpoint, are impressive.

To grasp what has happened, it is necessary to go back to February of 1961. That's when directors of 26 federal agencies—including Internal Revenue Service, FBI, Bureau of Narcotics, Bureau of Customs, Postal Inspectors —sat around a long table in a conference room at the Justice Department as the new attorney general, Robert Kennedy, discussed plans for what he called a "war on organized crime." To coordinate the "war," he said, the Justice Department's new Organized Crime Division would process information on racketeers, then refer each case to the appropriate government branch. Like the other government divisions, IRS agreed to give top priority to investigating men said to be syndicated criminals. The subsequent directive to IRS investigative personnel, signed by then-Commissioner Mortimer Caplin, stressed:

. . . I cannot emphasize too strongly the importance I attach to the success of the Service's contribution to this overall program . . . The tax returns of major racketeers to be identified by the Department of Justice will be subjected to the "saturation type" investigation, utilizing such man-power on each case as can be efficiently employed. In conducting such investigations, full use will be made of available electronic equipment and other technical aids, as well as such investigative techniques as surveillance, undercover work, etc.

In the following five years, the overall crusade resulted in a tenfold increase in convictions of racketeers. Significantly, Internal Revenue's investigators accounted for 64 percent—or 1,214 of the Justice Department's convictions (plus assessing $219 million in additional taxes)—even though 26 federal agencies participated in the anti-crime program. The statistics not only indicate that Internal Revenue's Intelligence Division is perhaps the government's most effective enforcement branch but lend considerable weight to Commissioner Sheldon Cohen's statement in 1965: "Without the wholehearted efforts of the Internal Revenue Service there could have been no organized crime drive nearly resembling that sponsored by the Administration and Congress since February of 1961."

Two reasons, apart from investigative skills, help ac-

count for Internal Revenue's effectiveness against the
Mafia. One, IRS need not prove a hoodlum's actual crime
of, say, trafficking in narcotics; but often can cause his
conviction for tax evasion with evidence that his standard
of living or accumulated wealth exceeds the income declared on his tax return. Two, organized criminals control
most illegal gambling operations and violate a law if they
don't pay federal taxes on the receipts. Both frequently
are interlocked.

Take, first, the net-worth theory. Developing proof that
a mobster spent more money than he reported as income
already requires about four times as many investigative
hours as a non-racketeer case and the task is growing
more strenuous. Now racketeers are totally conscious of
IRS's basic technique and employ accountants and lawyers to guard against self-incrimination. Additionally,
hoodlums no longer buy the biggest houses in areas where
they tend to concentrate such as Detroit's Grosse Point,
Chicago's Oak Park or River Forest, or even Gary, Indiana.

Yet numerous persons in Gary, for example, knew that a
61-year-old racketeer named Fred T. Mackey could well
afford the most expensive home in that steel mill city. He
controlled Gary's largest gambling operation—a racket
which local residents called the "Black and Gold Tornado
lottery"—but the challenge was, as had been since 1932,
to prove in court that Mackey received this money.

That is exactly what evidence gathered by the Indianapolis District Intelligence Division did in 1964. The
evidence was so solid that Mackey had evaded $994,340
in taxes on unreported income of $1,281,790 from 1956 to
1960 that his defense attorney's weak rebuttal is charac-

terized one by statement. "This," he said as the prosecutor displayed over 1,000 exhibits, "is a batch of scrambled Chinese chop suey." Far from being scrambled, the exhibits revealed that Mackey held assets in at least four other individuals' names; was the silent board chairman of Gibraltar Mutual Benefit Life Insurance Company and Gibraltar Industrial Life Insurance Company in Gary; and that even the two small insurance companies acquired property costing more than their gross receipts from premiums. Furthermore, a witness testified that Mackey had handed him nearly $150,000 in cash to invest and, upon questioning, added, "I nursed it all the way back to Atlanta." Then the witness admitted that he helped Mackey prepare a fictitious mortgage for $200,000 and that no money was exchanged in the "transaction." Mackey was sentenced to five years in prison and fined $50,000.

The Intelligence Division's oft-used weapon to trap mobsters on wagering tax violations stems from the federal government's earlier decision to pursue the illegal gambling business more for money than morality. Back in 1951, the House Ways and Means Committee, which drafts federal tax laws, searched for methods to raise additional taxes to meet the immense rise in government spending ($21.4 billion in 1951) for the Korean War. One answer arose from the late Senator Estes Kefauver's subcommittee to Investigate Organized Crime in Interstate Commerce. As mobsters were dramatically paraded before the televised hearings, the nation heard that "firmly entrenched organized criminal gangs" were "financed by big-time gambling." Since gambling receipts were untaxed—apart from wagering on legalized horse and dog racing and Nevada's gaming casinos—it seemed logical to tax all bets. Thus the Ways and Means Committee conceived legislation which it estimated would produce $400 million a year in federal taxes. Enacted November 1, 1951, the law compelled any bookmaker or numbers operator to register his illegal business at Internal Revenue's district office; buy an annual $50 occupational tax stamp for himself and every employee, plus a $250 stamp for each slot machine or coin-operated pinball machine on his premises; and to maintain daily records and forward 10 percent of his gross receipts to IRS.

Such gamblers, estimates the Department of Justice, gross about $7 billion a year in bets on sports events, pinball and slot machines, and the popular "numbers" or "policy" racket. "Policy," a name resulting from gamblers once siphoning off nickels that low-income families had budgeted for weekly premiums on insurance policies, today involves quarters and dollars but remains a semi-lottery: People seeking that perpetual "big killing" spend a quarter for a 1,000-to-1 chance to win $150—by simply picking a three-digit number that, hopefully, matches a designated series of numbers that will be published in a newspaper. The numbers may be the second, third and fourth numbers on the Dow-Jones stock-market averages or the total amount wagered at a racetrack. Each day millions of quarters and dollars go to "runners" who are well-known in their areas (the player must know where to find his runner if he "hits") and operate in factories, bars, tenement houses and offices, including, as an IRS raid illustrated, the labyrinthian Pentagon building's corridors. After deducting his 10 percent commission, the runner delivers his daily receipts to a "controller" or intermediary, who forwards the money to the "bank," a counting-house ruled by syndicated racketeers.

The extent of these numbers operations is best shown by court testimony: Tony Grosso, publicly called "Pittsburgh's numbers boss" before Internal Revenue agents caught him, estimated that between 1958 and 1963, he employed about 5,000 numbers writers and annually took in about $13 million at one operation alone. Myer Sigal, another gambler in Pittsburgh, estimated his annual receipts from numbers rackets totaled $3.5 million for each of the same years. A third operator, Henry Katz, testified that he grossed $2,184,000 a year. Additionally, enormous bets on sports events have become common. During the trial in 1965 of a bookmaker who posed as an accountant in a suburb of New York, evidence was presented that showed he had a $500 minimum for bets on football, basketball, baseball, boxing and elections. One of his leading clients testified that he personally bet $103,000 on a professional football game between the Green Bay Packers and the Chicago Bears. "Why we frequently find what's called a wire room, with two men, two phones and no crowds coming or going, that takes in $250,000 in a weekend," says William A. Kolar, IRS Director of Intelligence.

Yet in 1965 gamblers voluntarily bought only 7,284 of Internal Revenue's stamps and paid $7 million in gambling excise taxes, not the projected $400 million a year. ($1 million of the $7 million came from legalized gambling in Las Vegas and Reno, Nevada.) Specifically, in the 14 years from 1952 to 1966 a total of only $100 million was collected in gambling taxes and sales of stamps. Why? For one thing, the IRS gambling stamp doesn't license a gambling house but actually advertises the purchaser's illegal business to local governments and invites raids from scrupulous police. For another, dishonest police sometimes allow gamblers to operate without IRS stamps for payoffs much less than the 10 percent tax. Police have Constitutional jurisdiction to administer local antigambling laws, but, when gamblers are allowed to operate in violation of the wagering tax statutes, IRS can raid a gambler.

Often when IRS Intelligence agents do invade a bookmaker's quarters, they find both policemen and gamblers scrambling for windows. Consider, for example, Attorney General Nicholas Katzenbach's summary of the aforementioned Pittsburgh operations raided by IRS: "There was extensive documentation of the fact that police not only did not act against illegal gambling rings, but were paid to condone them. During Sigal's trial on wagering tax evasion charges, there was testimony to the effect that policemen were seen in Sigal's headquarters while the day's numbers were being counted up. All three of the gamblers I referred to admitted to paying large amounts to police, even five-figure amounts to a single police official . . . Meanwhile similar activity flourished in nearby New Kensington, Pa., where Sam Mannarino was operating open casinos and horse-betting rooms in the Garibaldi Building. We know this was done with acquiescence of city officials. When IRS agents raided the Mannarino establishment, they found three policemen on the premises. One was in uniform, but even he reflected some sensitivity. He had taken off his badge."

Since Internal Revenue has never received any extra agents specifically to enforce the gambling excise law, it cannot spend more than 15 percent of its manpower on betting activities without neglecting other investigations. This manpower must be well-budgeted. In fiscal 1965, the Intelligence Division made 1,734 preliminary investigations into gambling operations suspected of not having an IRS stamp or of evading excise taxes. Then such places often were scouted by undercover agents posing as inveterate gamblers, intoxicated sailors and conventioneers, or whatever disguise seemed appropriate. (In penetrating a bookmaker's tenement near New York City's Mt. Sinai Hospital, an agent wore a doctor's white coat as he nervously bet $40 on the first race at Aqueduct.) Next, after obtaining federal search warrants from the U.S. Commissioner's office, IRS personnel raided gambling establishments in most major cities, seized $1,187,000 in currency or gambling equipment, and recommended that 1,114 individuals be prosecuted.

These raids must be so synchronized that no gambler has time to destroy the incriminating betting or policy slips. If Internal Revenue's agents seize the slips, they usually can easily substantiate tax evasion charges. Accordingly, most gambling houses work behind double doors, one-way mirrors and hidden electronic warning systems. If gamblers hear agents yell, "federal agents— open up," they simply touch a lit cigarette to their betting slips that often are made from magician's flash paper or have been treated with nitrate cellulose and burn instantly, leaving no traceable ashes.*

But late the night of August 22, 1961, for instance, 35 Internal Revenue agents did not intend to allow the num-

---

* Gamblers who burned their fingers destroying evidence found a new paper on the market in 1965 that dissolves when dropped in water.

bers writers at the Sportsman's Club and adjoining liquor store in Newport, Kentucky, time to even grab a cigarette. Undercover agents had scouted the club for seven months and knew the layout perhaps as well as the architect. One agent had infiltrated the counting room, 34 others had encircled the building. And when the senior agent received a signal on his miniature transmitter, the S and S (search and seizure) would start. One group of agents would, if necessary, batter the strategic doors with sledge-hammers. A second wave would race in with either their .38 revolvers ready or carrying fire extinguishers. This was the only way the raid could work.

The Sportsman's, just may have been the nation's biggest illegal gambling club. Furthermore, surrounding Newport was unlike any other area. It was a vice-infested, grimy, Ohio River city with 33,000 people, narrow streets, two bridges across the Ohio River linking it to Cincinnati, and an apt nickname: The Gomorrah of America. It also was, at that time, the national layoff center, where syndicated gamblers set odds and point spreads on ball games and accepted "contra bets"—large bets that local bookies around the country were afraid to hold. There was little effort to hide anything. Much of Newport's local government had been so notoriously collusive that the Campbell County (Kentucky) Grand Jury subsequently indicted 13 members for allegedly conspiring to permit widespread vice.*

The Sportsman's Club did not share Newport's gambling traffic. After many of Newport's other gambling houses had been mysteriously bombed or burned out, the

* Additionally, the county sheriff, Norbert Roll, received a one-year sentence for failing to file an income tax return.

numbers operation was consolidated at the Sportsman's Club, Internal Revenue's senior agent pointed out when obtaining a federal search warrant. To attract business, the club offered the variety of a casino in Las Vegas. Its front room featured name entertainers, its back rooms contained slot machines, crap tables, beat-the-dealer, roulette, men taking bets on horse races and other sports events, plus day and night numbers games. These "winning" numbers, in contrast to most numbers operations, were dropped from a machine resembling those used in bingo games.

The money pouring into the Sportsman's went into so-called locked "drop boxes" and periodically was taken to a counting room with concealed annexes. This entire operation appeared to adhere to federal wagering tax laws. The club displayed one of Internal Revenue's $50 gambling tax stamps and in the previous 2½ years its management had mailed $119,637 to Internal Revenue as 10 percent of the reported gross receipts of $1,196,379. But, a subsequent indictment was to charge, the Sportsman's actual intake was $5,071,930 and its federal tax liabilities totaled $507,193. To prove this, IRS agents had to penetrate the secret rooms and outrace the gamblers to the betting slips. They also needed to grab records that could prove the Sportsman's Club was directed, not by the registered owners, but by Frank (Screw) Andrews. Often called the "numbers kingpin," Andrews had been arrested 46 times on charges starting with alleged murder and had spent 10 months in Atlanta's Federal Penitentiary on a previous gambling tax conviction.

At 11:30, Internal Revenue hit. Outside, agents wielding sledgehammers broke in the doors. Then came the move that would decide the raid's success or failure. An IRS undercover agent who had infiltrated the counting room as a club employee and radioed agents outside the building, opened the steel doors from inside the counting room. Five women employed at the numbers booth didn't have time to drop their ball-point pens. Many of the 175 customers screamed and raced unsuccessfully for exits, reminiscent of raids on Prohibition-era speakeasies. But, as soon as the crowd was checked by four agents to ascertain that none of the Sportsman's employees had slipped among them, everyone was released.

Then, systematically, agents searched each room for compartments concealed behind electrically operated walls. They found the secret rooms, and by 4 A.M., the agents had confiscated 17 adding machines, a duplicating machine, typewriter, microphone, three large safes (containing more than $50,000), blackboards listing odds on sports events, and box after box of numbers tickets. But the machine used to drop the "winning" numbers made the most forcible impression on the agents. "Look at this hidden compartment and special numbers," one agent observed disgustedly. "They can even rig the game."

Fifteen hours later, at 2:30 the next afternoon, the search and seizure had been completed. At 3 P.M., the second phase of the investigation began: 12 pairs of special agents, each equipped with blank grand jury subpoenas, interviewed over 200 employees or suspected participants at the Sportsman's Club, and obtained 53 witnesses for the Federal Grand Jury. Two of the five women employed on the night-shift numbers racket yielded invaluable evidence after a district judge threatened to hold them for contempt if they continued to invoke the Constitution's Fifth Amendment. Their testimony: The Sportsman's lowest average daily receipts from the day numbers racket was approximately $8,500 to $9,500, but that they had been told to do "government work" by pulling only $1,800 to $2,000 a day to be recorded for tax purposes. Surprisingly, the actual records were kept three days for what a supervisor called an "overlook," then destroyed.

Such testimony could be corroborated if the seized tickets were deciphered. After working three weeks, six agents from Internal Revenue had reassembled the tickets to substantiate the club's actual income. Two other special agents, in studying the Sportsman's Club's microfilmed bank records, detected a code on the back of the deposited checks that indicated the identity of the numbers writers who had accepted the check and turned in the deposits. Moreover, fast-working agents received an unexpected treasure of evidence. When they heard that the Sportsman's Club's adjacent liquor store was aflame, they drove there. Firemen quickly extinguished the fire and, at dawn, fire inspectors and IRS agents found pile after pile of clearly identifiable numbers tickets on the second floor where the fire originated.

The slips, seized as abandoned property, solidified the government's charges. Then the case was clinched when the prosecutor's 93rd and last witness, a handwriting analyst employed by IRS, testified that the confiscated records showing the Sportsman's Club's income for a five-week period could only be that of Frank (Screw) Andrews. On July 31, 1962, Andrews and seven associates each were sentenced to five years in prison and fined $10,000 on the first of 25 counts of gambling tax evasion. On other counts, the eight men were sentenced to a total of 765 years in prison and levied with $1,120,000 in back taxes and penalties.

The Sportsman's double doors and hidden rooms are standard shields against possible IRS raids at even smaller gambling houses that accept only sports bets and "policy." Besides this defense, most gambling establishments' locations are much less obvious. Perhaps the most common type of betting operation is what the trade calls a Jersey Pad. The operator, who does not buy a tax stamp, conceals himself in an apartment or behind a stationery store, installs a telephone and Princess extension, and works only by phone and through "pickup men" (couriers), leaving no suspicious procession of bettors.

While a telephone is, of course, the arm of the gambler's business, it frequently brings his demise. Internal Revenue's undercover agents often place bets to obtain a bookmaker's telephone number and, after getting that bookmaker's location from the telephone company, raid him. Or indebted horseplayers sometimes get revenge on pressuring bookies by telephoning IRS: "Check this number." But veteran gamblers such as one cool New Yorker, who shall be known here as Bronx Benny, insulate themselves against these traps. Thus when an undercover agent obtained the phone number that Benny used, the Manhattan Intelligence Division didn't locate the phone's site and break in the door. "All we'll find at this place is some lady cooking spaghetti," predicted Jack Wilson, the senior agent.

The agents sensed that Benny, who had not bought a tax stamp, also used the "back-strap" operation. He had. Benny paid a woman to attach an extension to her phone, then ran the wire through a window, across a fire escape and into an efficiency apartment that he rented during the day from a female narcotics addict. Now if IRS agents ever raided the owner of the telephone, they wouldn't find the bookie. By the time the back strap was traced, Benny would have left.

Instead, an IRS agent dressed in a plaid sport shirt squeezed through a trapdoor to the tar roof adjacent to the woman's apartment. Pretending to look for a lost ball, the agent wandered about and then dropped from his sleeve a ball which he picked up and tossed into the street. By now he had spotted the cord leading through a window to another apartment. Shortly afterwards three IRS agents were going through that window. In an unprecedented coincidence, two agents from the Bureau of Narcotics were pushing themselves through the apartment door. Bronx Benny and his assistant, both tucking telephones under their chin and scribbling on pads, were oblivious to the female addict and the male narcotic peddler passionately engaged on a rollaway bed.

After the Narcotics agents arrested the addicted lovemakers and Internal Revenue agents arrested the bookies, two other IRS agents began answering the ringing telephones and pretended to accept bets in order to testify later how much business the gamblers transacted. "O.K. six for 99," an agent would say, repeating the courier's code word. Or: "O.K. bushel for basket." "Frank for I.D.? O.K. ten across, 2–2 at Garden. You're on."

As soon as Internal Revenue agents perforate a gambler's technique, however, new methods emerge. One is what bookmakers call the cheese-box technique. Instead of splicing onto another person's telephone, gamblers have a phone installed in a room, then attach to it an electronic device that is so named because it usually is fitted inside a Velveeta wooden cheese box. Then the bookie leaves the site of the phone and stations himself blocks away in another room with a phone attached to a similar cheese box. Consequently, when a bettor dials the number of the phone in the empty room, the bookie pushes a button on the cheese box in Room No. 2 and takes the call. The beauty of the cheese-box apparatus, from a bookie's standpoint, is that if IRS agents locate the telephone used to transmit bets, all they find is a phone and cheese box. No cords lead agents to the bookie.

A sophisticated improvement over the cheese box, called the blue-box attachment and carrying ominous overtones, was discovered in use near Miami, Florida, in late 1965. A 5-by-12-inch instrument that resembles a small adding machine, the blue box not only enables gamblers to operate several phones from concealed locations, but it also allows them to dial the area code of another city by pushing a button, thereby bypassing all the telephone company's mechanism that times calls and compiles toll charges. Thus gambling syndicates can make hundreds of long-distance calls each month without being charged or have their volume of calls arouse suspicion in a telephone company.

Ostensibly, it would appear that organized gamblers hold a technological advantage over IRS investigators. Not entirely. Internal Revenue personnel receive information from telephone companies, whose instruments often can detect among innumerable things, a cheese-box operation. And even without such equipment, IRS special agents have yet to find an impenetrable gambling establishment. In Buffalo, New York, an active betting district,

IRS agents located one bookmaking operation that calmly worked behind electronic warning systems and two reinforced steel doors—a barricade that would resist any raiders not supported by a tank. But agents chopped through the roof and caught the bookmaker before he could hang up all three of his phones.

As impressive as the Intelligence Division's record of oppressing gamblers and racketeers may be, it must be appraised as a regulatory effect and a negligible tax-collecting measure. A year's yield from criminals is only enough revenue to finance the federal government for a little more than two hours. In some ways, the anticrime drive costs IRS, for the House Ways and Means Committee once calculated that an agent assigned to the racketeer drive averages collecting about $46,000 a year in additional taxes and penalties while an agent handling conventional audit or fraud cases brings in an average of $184,000 per year. Explicitly, Internal Revenue cannot forget that it is a collection agency and, therefore, is often only slightly less intense in chasing the more numerous and characteristic evaders like the traveling salesman who keep moving to avoid paying $145 in overdue taxes. Now we reach the point where Internal Revenue pursues the so-called average American who swears he cannot pay his taxes.

8

Adult Delinquency

Revenue officer Sol Stein was a stout, black-haired man wearing a gray mohair suit and maroon tie. He did not know what his target looked like. All he knew was that the DA (delinquent account)—an itinerant construction worker whom we'll call Leon Neff—had ignored three of Internal Revenue's bills and finally a notice ordering him to appear at the Manhattan district office and explain why he hadn't paid $88.62 in overdue taxes. Accordingly, Stein was now bending over the mailboxes in the lobby of a brick apartment building in the Bronx, New York, looking for Neff's name. He did not find the name, so he pulled out his wallet and looked at the attached note pad. "2B," he noted, then pushed the button marked "2B." The electric lock on the lobby door buzzed, the IRS officer entered and saw a tall, wavy-haired man in a sports shirt poised in the apartment's doorway. "Mr. Leon Neff?" he asked.

"Who's that again?" the man responded.

"Leon Neff."

"Oh, oh, the fellow who used to live here," the man recalled. "Naw, they say he's up in Canada someplace looking for work."

"I don't reckon you know whereabouts in Canada he lives?" the revenue officer replied.

"No telling," the man said, shaking his head for emphasis. "Never find that man."

"No relatives or anybody who might know his address?" Stein said slowly, purposely stalling until he saw two grammar-school girls emerge from another apartment. He stopped talking, leaving the man an alternative of either volunteering information or speaking to the girls. The man nodded perfunctorily and said, "How you girls today?"

"Fine, thank you, Mr. Neff," the oldest girl said.

"You're my man," Stein said to the clearly disconcerted Leon Neff. "And I'll have to collect $88.62 or confiscate equitable assets."

"And I ain't letting this TV set go," interjected a woman, presumably Neff's wife, from another room. Stein got the money.

Every day, every hour from 8:30 A.M. to midnight, Revenue officers are in comparable doorways, apartments, banks, loan companies, and businesses' cashiers' offices making what the Internal Revenue Service manual defines as "enforced collections" and employees often call "nailing deadbeats." Such work, not part of the Audit or Intelligence process, is the job of the Collection Division's Delinquent Accounts & Returns Branch. Often it's called "DAR" and not for, as some employees like to joke, "the Daughters of the American Revolution." Neither are these officers little-old-lady personalities. They are tenacious men (and sometimes women) whose work is similar to that of finance-company collectors. So similar, in fact, that the tax collector's title was changed from "revenue collector" to "revenue officer" in order to avoid the connotation of loan companies' muscular enforcers. Still, the name "revenue officer" doesn't mean, as IRS Commissioner Sheldon Cohen has said, that Internal Revenue is "becoming a lenient creditor."

The agents probably have more delinquent bills to collect than perhaps all finance companies have each year. In 1965, a reasonably typical year, all of Internal Revenue's DAR branches closed out 2.8 million delinquent accounts that owed $1.5 billion in taxes and penalties. Yet, at the end of 1965, Internal Revenue listed an inventory of 530,000 individuals and businesses owing $1.3 billion in uncollected delinquent taxes and interest, and wrote off $328.3 million as "uncollectable delinquent accounts." Large as the figure may seem, it is the lowest since 1945 and reflects that IRS collectors are winning the battle against delinquency. At the end of fiscal 1955, Internal Revenue had a backlog of 1,549,000 persons who owed $1.6 billion in unpaid taxes.

A nontaxpayer, or taxpayer, is classified as a tax delinquent for a variety of reasons: He may not have filed a return; filed but didn't pay any or all of his taxes due; paid with a worthless check; was audited and didn't pay the additional assessment; or, as IRS personnel say, "missed the 10-day cycle." The cycle means that anyone who doesn't pay a bill from Internal Revenue within 10 days after it is mailed eventually is categorized as "delinquent." Such a strict computerized billing system, it should be noted before proceeding, also brands thousands of persons as "delinquent" even though they really aren't delinquent. Illustrative is the case of an insurance agent who, after paying his taxes, received a bill for $28.11 and a printed form called "Notice of Error in Arithmetic." After verifying the accuracy of his calculations on an adding machine, he typed a letter to Internal Revenue asking, "Why do I owe this?" Twenty-one days later he received a notice reminding him of severe penalties for nonpayment. After 34 days he received a printed postcard that stated: "Your letter will be answered as soon as possible."

Next came another bill demanding $28.11 plus an additional one-half percent monthly interest. Then arrived a printed form stating that, since he had not paid, he would have to report to an IRS officer between 10 A.M. and noon on a designated day. A concession stated that if he paid before the appointed date, he would not have to appear. He paid, removing himself from the delinquent status, but never knowing exactly why he was on the list in the first place. After 71 days, he received as an answer to his letter a printed form with a "X" beside this sentence: "Error in computation of dividends received credit, retirement income credit, investment credit or other credits." He had taken none of those credits.

Most individuals and businesses categorized as delinquent, however, know why they are being billed and are unmistakably delinquent. Usually they disregard all bills for overdue taxes and finally their summons to appear at an Internal Revenue office and explain why they cannot pay the taxes. (An explanation that a person cannot pay a tax bill seldom suffices; often an IRS employee directs the individual to where he can get a loan to pay the tax.)

Furthermore, a contemptuous minority of Americans, undaunted by IRS's grim publicity about tax dodgers, must be forced to file a return. Each May, June and July, IRS Collection Divisions use manual and computer methods to determine if most persons who filed a return the previous year have submitted a return for the current year. Then after eliminating non-filers who have retired, died, married or are no longer earning enough money to file, Revenue officers pressure individuals and businesses to file about 1.2 million returns and pay $220.2 million in taxes and interest. In such instances, IRS's leverage is 6 percent annual interest plus fines going up to 50 percent of the unpaid taxes or eventual confiscation of property.

Such non-filers range from maids to small manufacturers. "Non-filers also vary from place to place," as has been said by an official in the National Office's Collection Division. "In one area it may be the small general store or filling station operator. In another, it may be the subcontractor or itinerant entrepreneur who goes around picking up odd jobs. Elsewhere, many of the used-car dealers may give us trouble."

Just as much trouble frequently comes from some businessmen who do file. Take the common ploy used by a dress contractor located in Manhattan's Seventh Avenue garment district. Every three months he withheld over $18,000 from employees' wages for income tax and Social Security payments but forwarded less than $200 to Internal Revenue.* Then each quarter, after ignoring all of IRS's notices, he would pay the $18,000 only after an IRS

---

* Internal Revenue still allows employees credit for taxes withheld, even if the employer doesn't forward it to IRS, on grounds that such manipulation is no fault of the taxpayer.

officer appeared at his business with a paper called NO-TICE OF SEIZURE. Finally, he grew bolder. The fourth time an IRS collector appeared to seize the business, the owner, personally wealthy but unexplainably refusing to surrender the withholding taxes, swore that he had mailed the money. As proof that he had mailed the payment, he offered to call the *New York Times* to urge an exposé on the incredibly slow postal system. The mail never brought the dressmaker's check. Thus the Revenue officer taped a NOTICE OF SEIZURE on the door, closing the business. Then, after allowing the dressmaker 10 days to pay the $18,000 in overdue taxes, the same IRS officer auctioned off the business equipment, although he realized that the sale would net only about $300 after paying off preferred creditors. But the move enabled IRS to invoke a power that the dressmaker apparently didn't realize existed: levy a 100 percent penalty on the remaining debt of $17,700, making the total due $35,400 and confiscate the employer's personal assets.

Even employees can be just as problematic. Consider a pretentious man employed by a trade association and having all the symptoms of a tax delinquent: problems with seven creditors and his wife, plus a 21-year-old bleached-blonde secretary who giggled at his jokes and made him forget his next birthday would be No. 40. In order to maintain his facade as a semi-affluent playboy, he did not arrange to have sufficient taxes withheld from his salary and, naturally, could not pay the $286 taxes that came due on April 15. Neither did he pay when billed each subsequent month; nor did he keep his appointment at IRS. By December, his account had been assigned to a revenue officer for collection, but the agent found the man had no worthwhile assets to confiscate. The mortgage on his house, automobile and furniture totaled more than his equity. Thus, after the man ignored the FINAL NOTICE BEFORE SEIZURE, the revenue officer filled out a paper called NOTICE OF LEVY, confiscated the man's Christmas bonus of $315 and had the balance, $14 after interest, mailed to the man's home.

Internal Revenue's broad authority to confiscate money and property is its simplest way to collect delinquent accounts. An IRS collector doesn't need a court's permission to make a seizure. He merely writes the nontaxpayer's name on the aforementioned forms NOTICE OF LEVY (to seize money) or NOTICE OF SEIZURE (to confiscate property), and takes any assets that he can find. Nothing appears too trivial to confiscate. In at least three instances, a Senate subcommittee has found, Internal Revenue agents have seized as little as two or three dollars in special checking accounts. While confiscations seldom meet the amount of tax liability, they do cause Internal Revenue to collect a variety of assets. Consider some the Service held in 1965:

• The football helmets, shoulder pads and uniforms, plus contracts of 33 players owned by the former Providence (Rhode Island) Steamrollers in the Atlantic Coast Football League. The team was seized in order to settle what Internal Revenue said was a debt of $4,700.98 in withholding and excise taxes.

• A printing press, swastika arm bands, Nazi flags, framed pictures of Adolf Hitler and other paraphernalia in a two-story frame house in Arlington, Virginia, that had been rented by George Lincoln Rockwell and his American Nazi Party. The Nazis allegedly owed $5,000 in taxes.

• Three handsome Belgian plow horses owned by Valentine Byler, a farmer and one of 18,000 members of the Amish religious colony who haven't changed their austere method of living since migrating from Europe to Maryland and Pennsylvania in the 18th century. The Amish pay income taxes but refuse to pay Social Security taxes (nor accept its benefits) on grounds that it is an insurance and thereby violates their faith in God's will. Even after Byler's horses were auctioned for $460, or $37.89 more than his tax bill, he refused to accept a check refunding the balance.

Horses, too, can demonstrate how Internal Revenue's collectors occasionally will take a sporting chance and postpone a seizure. A classic example resulted in Los Angeles when a Revenue officer was unable to collect approximately $100,000 owed by a well-known actor. Then the officer read that the actor's horse was heavily favored to win a $20,000 race at Santa Anita Race Track. He drove to the track, and, seconds after the horse won by an easy three lengths, eased into the winner's circle and told the jubilant actor that he had confiscated both the horse and winning purse. The actor's lawyer, quick to point out how easily the horse won, persuaded the tax collector not to seize the $20,000, but to allow them to use it to fly the horse to either Monmouth Park Race Track in New Jersey or Aqueduct in New York, where he was certain to win a stake race that would gross over $100,000. Since Internal Revenue would collect the actor's entire debt if the horse won, the Service took the gamble. Like most horseplayers, however, the IRS lost its $20,000 bet. The horse finished sixth.

Internal Revenue's most difficult collection cases result,

of course, when the tax delinquent appears to have no salable property to confiscate. Therefore, such situations dictate, in some District Collection Divisions' viewpoint, that any legal means be employed to secure the money. One basic technique is for group supervisors to give Revenue officers spirited lectures without using Internal Revenue's taboo phrases such as "quota" or "production basis." The officers are evaluated on the number of delinquent cases they close and, naturally, a case cannot be closed without collecting money. As a former IRS agent in Massachusetts has described the system: "They look in your bag each month to see how much you've got."

Thus any ambitious agent knows that a consistently full bag can mean an increase in salary. One enterprising collection method alone brought a promotion for Revenue Officer H. A. Groves, according to testimony by Allen N. Brunwasser, an attorney from Pittsburgh, before a Senate subcommittee in 1965. Brunwasser testified that his client witnessed Groves station himself inside a shoe repair shop on which the proprietor owed taxes and, each time a customer picked up his repaired shoes and started to pay, the IRS officer showed a NOTICE OF LEVY and confiscated the $2.69, the $3.25, *et cetera*. (Always, Brunwasser added, Groves was courteous and, at the end, told the shoe cobbler that he could seek a compromise with IRS on the amount owed.)

If Internal Revenue's collection methods seem unduly rigid, it must be remembered that, like policemen patrolling areas such as Harlem or Times Square and often meeting contempt, many IRS officers deal with people who don't fail to use their own blatant techniques. At the bottom level, the Revenue officer's beat is a world of mendacious tax delinquents in which a truthful answer or forwarding address would astonish him. Consider frequent situations that IRS officers encounter:

Item: A tax collector on Chicago's South Side asked a plump woman where her husband could be located. "That son-of-a-bitch's run away with some young girl," the wife answered. When the Revenue officer noticed a pair of men's muddy shoes were sitting on a newspaper, he asked, "Aren't those your husband's shoes?" "No sir! on a stack of Bibles," she replied. "They—well, if that son-of-a-bitch can get him a young girl I sure'n hell can get me a man." The "new man" was, of course, her tax-dodging husband.

Item: When an officer told an owner of a laundry in Manhattan that he had come to collect a 17-month-old tax debt, the laundryman said: "Sir, I've turned over all my records and my checks to an accountant in the Empire State Building." After establishing that no such accountant ever occupied that address, the tax collector returned to the laundry and was told testily: "If the accountant has run away with my records and money, that's your tough luck."

Item: A tax collector located a musician in the Far West and identified himself as an Internal Revenue officer. Excusing himself, the banjo player returned to the telephone, then screamed, "Oh, lord, my wife's been hit by a car!" He raced out, leaving the door open, and yelling: "Hospital! Gotta get to the hospital!" He had never been married.

Then there are countless tax delinquents who attempt what Revenue officers call a Number Six. These cases often begin under circumstances like those on the morning of May 17, 1957. Until that time, an IRS officer had been trying to collect $3,789 owed in taxes for a four-year period by a salesman. Suddenly, only a few days after the salesman was mailed a FINAL NOTICE BEFORE SEIZURE, he was reported drowned while ignoring storm warnings and fishing alone in Lake Erie. His rented motorboat was found overturned on a rocky shore and, while his body was never recovered, he was ruled legally dead by a municipal court. Unfortunately, he left a wife pregnant with their fourth child.

In February, 1965, a resident of the same town was meandering through a sports show in Chicago and was startled to see this same salesman, his late acquaintance. The salesman was wearing a black eye-patch and was billed as a champion sportsman, under another name. Upon inquiry he insisted he was a television sportscaster and had never been a salesman. His wife, a photographer's model whom he married in 1961, agreed. The upshot? He was indeed the missing salesman, identified by his two brothers, his first wife and fingerprints on his service records. And, in 1966, a county probate court declared him officially alive. But the six-year statute of limitations on collecting income taxes had expired.

Another type of tax delinquents are persons whom society recognizes as outstanding citizens and who are, in essence, the disputers. Such individuals avoid the probability of having IRS confiscate and publicly auction their property by disputing the amount of taxes owed. Probably the most ironical illustration, though the technique is common, has been Franklin D. Roosevelt, Jr., son of the President who began heavy federal taxation. Among the $26,000 in unpaid taxes that IRS Collection Division attempted to obtain from Roosevelt was a tax of $12,647 on income of $18,615.21 received in 1958 as Roosevelt's share of the receipts from *Sunrise at Campobello,* a Broadway drama about FDR's affliction with polio. The younger Roosevelt, later Under Secretary of Commerce, insisted that the money was nontaxable "compensation" for damages to his reputation. Not until October, 1964, when IRS's rejection of the claim was upheld by the U.S. Tax Court, could IRS attempt to collect from Roosevelt. There was little doubt that the $18,615 was income and not for damages, emphasized Judge A. H. Pierce. The younger Roosevelt (and his family) approved playwright Dore Schary's finished script without seeking changes, and was only seven years old during the incident which was portrayed, therefore suffering no "loss of character, reputation or personal dignity."

The Service got the money. It almost always does, except when cases such as that of Joe Louis, the boxer who owed $1.1 million in delinquent taxes, are declared "uncollectable" or "not worth the effort to pursue." Despite the multitude of legal and illegal delaying tactics, IRS's bill collectors have a rate of proficiency that would embarrass any high-pressure loan company. Even in many seemingly lost causes, a Revenue officer points out, Internal Revenue usually grabs at least a fraction of the overdue taxes. One area in which Internal Revenue collectors consistently obtain a share of the delinquent tax bill, if they are alert, is in bankruptcy cases. Bankruptcies, which disturbingly have risen in the United States from 59,044 in 1955 to 180,323 in fiscal 1965, allow a hopelessly indebted person to legally discharge all liabilities and for creditors to salvage any remaining assets. Internal Revenue has priority claim on any remaining assets, usually a man's last paycheck from a job, but it sometimes requires initiative to get that check.

Such initiative came one Friday when a Revenue officer in Chicago learned that a salesman whom he had been chasing was about to file a voluntary petition of bankruptcy. Noting, too, that Friday was payday, the officer immediately drove to the appliance firm where the salesman worked, only to be told by a female cashier: "He has just left our employ and premises with his last paycheck." After a slight pause, the girl added, "Some of our people cash their checks at the liquor store on the corner."

Racing down the block, the tax collector found his man endorsing the paycheck and a clerk handing over a carton of Camels and two fifths of Jim Beam. After identifying himself, the IRS officer found that the check not only was large enough to cover the delinquent tax bill but left enough for the whiskey, cigarettes and $8 in pocket money. Still, the irate salesman's reaction was similar to a quip that IRS collectors often hear and insert in their interoffice circular: "I don't know who'll be our first man on the moon. But I sure as hell know who'll be second. He'll be the Internal Revenue tax collector." A few million other nontaxpayers might share that opinion.

Surprisingly, Internal Revenue already stations tax collectors virtually every place but the moon.

9

IRS's Man in Manila—and Elsewhere

A revenue agent in Internal Revenue's Manhattan District Office had just finished reviewing a businessman's return without finding any new irregularities. But he was intrigued by the expenses listed for rent, equipment, and salaries for several branch offices sprinkled across South America. Thus, the agent sensed, if the suspect had diverted funds to avoid taxes, a remote foreign subsidiary would be a natural source. The businessman had correctly surmised that Internal Revenue wouldn't send someone to South America to verify an office's existence. But he overlooked one point: The man from Internal Revenue was already in South America, working from the IRS office in the American Consulate in São Paulo, Brazil. And a week after the São Paulo office received a letter asking it for a "picture" of the New Yorker's costly foreign branch, the agent had his answer. The first "office" was a closet-size room with neither telephone nor furniture.

While most foreign-based American branch offices and

subsidiaries are not, of course, phony tax gimmicks, they often can be as accessible to Internal Revenue's scrutiny as firms with Wall Street addresses. Today, Internal Revenue's 533-man Office of International Operations (OIO) maintains miniature branches in Manila, Tokyo, London, Paris, Rome, Bonn, Ottawa, Mexico City, San Juan, and São Paulo; an even smaller office in Pago Pago, Samoa; and mobile agents who visit 118 foreign cities a year. Few areas in the free world are beyond Internal Revenue's reach. "We're equipped—after getting permission from the country involved—to help our taxpayers fill out their forms or to assist a district office to make a personal audit, investigation or collection almost anywhere except maybe Timbuktu," says William Shulman, veteran assistant to the OIO director.

Indeed Internal Revenue needs to function literally everywhere. Americans live almost everywhere—including two in Timbuktu, the fabled Saharan oasis that symbolizes the end of nowhere. At last count, 2.3 million American citizens lived overseas, giving the United States more residents on foreign soil than Great Britain had at the height of its colonial empire. These foreign-based Americans include 942,538 members of the armed forces and 603,550 dependents of servicemen and the Defense Department's civilian employees. The remainder are employed by federal agencies such as the State Department; or are private businessmen, corporation executives, employees on merchant vessels, construction projects and oil drillings, plus missionaries, doctors, teachers, technicians, reporters, actors, stenographers, students, drifters and daydreamers. Many work for the 20,000 American-owned overseas plants and businesses (value: $51 billion) that are centered along Germany's Ruhr and in London's suburbs, but stretch from Northern Ireland to the Congo's mining regions.

All of these Americans must file income tax returns. Those with a legal address in the United States can mail their returns to the appropriate IRS district office. Overseas Americans without addresses in the United States send their returns—and in 1965 there were 448,353 such returns—to the OIO's four-story headquarters in northwest Washington, D.C. Both categories, though, encounter an employee from a foreign-based OIO office if their return becomes delinquent, is audited, or is suspected of being fraudulent. In 1965, for example, OIO's employees chased down 18,753 delinquent accounts and collected $6.4 million; and its auditors examined 22,104 returns, assessing an additional $57.9 million, or an average of $2,619 more per return, a rate three times higher than on audited returns of United States residents.

American businesses located in the United States and foreigners who sometimes have never seen the United States also come under OIO's jurisdiction. Internal Revenue district offices dealing with business returns that show income from overseas transactions periodically ask that OIO's employees audit the returns. In 953 of these examinations between 1963 and 1964 OIO auditors imposed additional taxes of $386.7 million, an average of *nearly $406,000 per case!* In a reverse situation, Internal Revenue collects taxes from foreigners who receive income from sources in the United States. IRS had corporations withhold $103.6 million from the $727.8 million in stock dividends and bank interest that was paid to nonresident aliens in 1965. Then OIO's overseas agents collected another $12.7 million from foreigners, though usually first asking permission from their governments. Otherwise such a collection could provoke a political furor. Just imagine how Americans would react if Italian and French tax collectors were pursuing Americans in Pennsylvania?

International operations often involve other entangled situations, a fact conceded in the Commissioner of Internal Revenue's annual report for 1965 on OIO duties: "Added to the full-range of audit and collection activity are many special problems not usually encountered in domestic rulings." One such basic intricacy arises from the question of what country has taxation jurisdiction on foreign-based Americans' income and how much? While the United States and most major nations maintain reciprocal tax treaties to minimize double taxation, many persons remain confused. An American who pays 16 percent of his income to, say, Belgium might believe that he has no further tax liability. Ordinarily, he would not pay more if his tax rate was 16 percent. But if his tax rate in the United States is 28 percent, he is permitted to deduct Belgium's 16 percent tax and pay 12 percent to Internal Revenue.

More complexity stems from legislation that exempts some foreign-based Americans' income. Further confusing the issue are enterprising Americans who fully utilize all opportunities. Consider, for example, a case decided in 1965 in which OIO agents used the net-expenditure theory to estimate that one overseas American (court name: Robida) had adjusted gross profits of $134,000 over a five-year period. Robida's profession? According to his brief filed in U.S. Tax Court, Robida became so proficient at tilting and thereby defeating slot machines at U.S. military installations in Japan that he soon began instructing soldiers and sailors to do two things: "To diagnose and manipulate the slot machines . . . to beat the game of gambling itself, hence breaking the addiction to it generally. To beat the element of chance and to make a profit for themselves by their skill and knowledge." Robida, who took a share of his trainees' winnings, became so successful that he employed a female assistant and then gave lessons in 100 service clubs in Japan, Okinawa, Taiwan, the Philippines, Morocco, Spain, France and Germany.

After Robida was arrested in Germany, Internal Revenue's agents began ferreting out how much he spent for hotels and plane fare and arrived at the five-year income of $134,000. When asked for records to prove or disprove the figure, Robida's eventual answers resembled an episode from either a James Bond movie or *McHale's Navy*, the farcical television series. Records? Hell, he was lucky to be alive. One devoted trainee had even tried to kill him by rigging an outdoor camping stove to explode. Then German authorities had seized all of his records. Robida didn't deny that he reaped huge profits from manipulating slot machines. But he claimed in a brief that at least $84,000 of his income was tax-exempt on grounds that it qualified as "compensation for personal services actually rendered. . . ." The Tax Court upheld Internal Revenue's position that Robida's profits came from a joint business venture and were thereby taxable.

Another investigation made overseas resulted in the largest tax lien that IRS ever placed against an individual. It all began when IRS's San Francisco District office referred the dossier of a John A. T. Galvin to OIO. Born in Hobart, Australia, Galvin became a newspaper reporter in

155

China during the 1930's, then settled in Hong Kong after World War II and discreetly acquired an estimated $150 million in what was reported to be mining and shipping. From 1954 to 1960, Galvin lived in and out of California, flamboyantly attracting attention from both the local society columnists and Internal Revenue office. He entertained lavishly at his 35,000-acre ranch in Santa Barbara, donated land to Stanford University, saw his daughter, Trish, selected for the U.S. Olympic riding team, and amused party guests with tales about his Far East adventures. One story frequently attributed to Galvin was how he allegedly began to amass his fortune: peddling calcium compound to Borneo's natives as a cure for diarrhea.

When contacted by Internal Revenue about his income during 1954–57, Galvin's attorney raised the primary issue that Galvin hadn't lived in California sufficient time to be liable for U.S. income or gift taxes. Anyway, Galvin had by now moved his family and horses to Dublin, Ireland. But agents from OIO's Manila office were meticulously reconstructing Galvin's trips to the Far East during the disputed period. They reviewed records of Galvin's Eastern Mining and Metals Co., Ltd., in Malaysia, then checked dates of contracts and airline and hotel records from Singapore to Hong Kong. After receiving these reports, Internal Revenue filed liens against Galvin's property in California for $21,261,818 in taxes and interest. Galvin protested the case in U.S. Tax Court, but settled with Internal Revenue in 1965 for *$12 million.*

There is no knowing how many entrepreneurs' overseas earnings go untaxed. Yet while Internal Revenue successfully reconstructs the affairs of a Robida or Galvin across four continents to collect taxes, it can fumble a case that arrives by mail. That is precisely what occurred when Charles E. Lehigh, an accountant for a Gulf Oil Company subsidiary in Venezuela, won $269,413 for a $2.39 ticket on a sports pool. Lehigh asked in a letter to Internal Revenue if the winnings qualified as income for personal services and therefore (at that time) were nontaxable? Although the winnings were taxable, Internal Revenue did not answer. A year later IRS mailed Lehigh a bill for $246,013 in taxes, but misaddressed the envelope, causing it to be returned. Five years later (1960) when Lehigh and his family returned to their home in El Dorado, Arkansas, Internal Revenue sued him for $303,226 in taxes, interest and penalties—or $6,813 more than he won. In pleading his own defense, Lehigh simply contended that IRS had not given him proper notice. Federal Judge J. Smith Henley ruled that Lehigh was right, IRS was wrong. Thus IRS could not collect the tax.

Not all Americans who receive money while abroad—or from foreign sources—bother to write to the Internal Revenue Service. Consequently, OIO personnel attempt to identify U.S. citizens who hold stock in overseas firms, quietly work in a foreign country; or small foreign businesses controlled by Americans who have conveniently forgotten about Internal Revenue. OIO officers have developed a productive starting point. They receive photocopies of all passport applications from the State Department and lists of stockholders from many European firms. These and other means have enabled OIO agents to identify 14,000 Americans owning 5 percent or more stock in 26,000 foreign corporations; then the information is forwarded to the taxpayers' district offices to verify if the income was included on their returns. Agents' inquisitiveness has been a valuable asset in locating American-owned businesses overseas. In their thoroughness, OIO agents have found Americans owned a profitable restaurant in South Africa, a small tramp ship plying the Far East, and even an "export" firm in Hong Kong that another branch of the United States government had envisioned could not be identified as an American enterprise: It was a front for the Central Intelligence Agency's covert operations.

Often forgetful Americans claim a plausible alibi: "I didn't know I had to pay taxes." Until 1963, Americans who lived outside the United States for more than 510 days didn't have to pay any American taxes on income from personal services. And businesses that didn't transfer profits back into the United States were exempt from all American taxes. But the exemption was so publicly exhibited by expatriate actors during the 1950's and early 1960's that it nearly helped destroy Hollywood as the motion picture capital and provoked Congress to revolutionize tax liabilities for Americans (or individuals who earn most of their living in the United States) living abroad. First Ava Gardner established her legal residence in Madrid. Then Elizabeth Taylor, Audrey Hepburn, Mel Ferrer, Gregory Peck, Yul Brynner, William Holden, Van Johnson, and Charlie Chaplin (who also left the United States owing Internal Revenue an alleged $1.2 million in taxes) established legal residence in houses they called chalets and villas in Switzerland's Alps thereby specifically avoiding U.S. taxes. Accordingly, the Elizabeth Taylor–Richard Burton team, for example, were not obligated to pay American income taxes on their salaries from the movie *Cleopatra*. Nor did Holden need to pay U.S. taxes on his estimated $2 million income from *The Bridge over the River Kwai.* Holden, furthermore, not only became known as a wealthy man from this adroitness but adopted the most pious attitude. "I would not budge," Holden said one day at his 15-room lake-front villa near Lausanne, Switzerland, "even if taxes in the United States were the same."

Swiss taxes, to be sure, were not the same; they were both negligible and negotiable. A person merely contacted the tax collector in a few of Switzerland's 22 cantons (states) until he found the lowest tax rate. He might call himself the Bill Holden Corporation and pay only two-tenths of 1 percent corporation tax on his profits and no tax on undistributed profits. And no law forced him to distribute profits. Or an American could reach an agreement to pay a tax of 5 percent on his monthly rent bill.

But the Revenue Acts of 1962 and 1964 drastically modified the exemption. Now an American citizen (except U.S. government employees) who lives outside the United States for a full calendar year and shows a tangible intent to remain there can subtract a maximum of $20,000 of his salary, plus the usual deductions for dependents and medical expenses, then pay taxes on any balance.* After three consecutive years of residence in a foreign country, the tax-exempt ceiling rises to $25,000, but the sum must include the value of all fringe benefits received such as the use of a house, automobile or club facilities. (The fringe-benefit clause moved one man to

* An American receives this exemption even if he lives in Tijuana, Mexico, a five-minute drive from California, or on the Canadian side of the Niagara Falls and only a three minute walk across the Rainbow Bridge to New York.

telephone an Internal Revenue office and ask: "Do you have to include the cost of meals and lodging received while in jail?")

This new limitation, mostly touching the few upper-income individuals or movie set, included two concessions to soften the tax. The maximum tax rate on individual income subsequently was lowered from 91 to 70 percent, and anyone whose annual earnings fluctuate was permitted to average the income over a seven-year period. Still some American movie personalities legally ceased being Americans and were absolved of paying any taxes to Internal Revenue. Among the first to legally renounce his American citizenship was John Huston, Missouri-born director of such movies as *The Misfits*. He chose to live in Ireland for what he called the "Irish pleasantries," which include minuscule rates of taxation. A more convenient would-be renunciation was taken by Elizabeth Taylor, who was born in England of American parents and thereby held both United States and British citizenships. After the overseas tax amendment was enacted, the actress said that she had renounced her American citizenship. And, since Britain doesn't tax its citizens who live abroad more than 183 days in a year, she could painlessly file an income tax return with Britain's Inland Revenue Board. Nevertheless, the Internal Revenue Service would tax Miss Taylor on any salary earned while she worked in the United States. Again, she and husband Richard Burton could legally circumvent most of these taxes when they starred in *The Sandpiper*, a scenic movie set in Carmel, California's Big Sur country. While the movie's exteriors were filmed in California, the Taylor-Burton team insisted that most of their scenes be filmed in Paris. Then they flew to California for *The Sandpiper*'s premiere.

Though expatriate American actors gained the most notoriety for tax avoidance, their total revenue was inconsequential in comparison to profits from American-owned foreign subsidiaries and businesses. Several such subsidiaries, though, have reacted similarly to Internal Revenue's new taxation on any profits of a foreign-based company in which American ownership is more than 50 percent. Inevitably, some Americans transferred enough of their stock to reduce holdings to 49 percent. Those persons, therefore, opened a new challenge to Internal Revenue's expanded OIO branches: to determine if such persons actually own only 49 percent or still effectively control the majority stock.

Simultaneously another of Internal Revenue's overseas responsibilities—trying to detect U.S. currency illegally flowing abroad—has enlarged in scope. Taxes on foreign-based American firms, IRS's drive on organized crime, and publicized campaigns against tax cheaters have increased traffic of unreported income to two sanctuaries for tax evaders: the Bahamas-to-Switzerland route. Take Britain's semi-autonomous Bahama Islands that lie only 81 miles off Florida and have no treaties agreeing to furnish any tax information about Americans to Internal Revenue. Instead, the Bahamas have suddenly prospered as a shadowy gambling and money haven.* Today, a syndicated

---

* In fact, three indicted gamblers from New York, Frank Ritter (alias Red Reed), Morris Schmertzler (alias Max Courtney) and Charles Brudner (alias Charlie Brud) operate the Monte Carlo Room Casino in Nassau's Lucayan Beach Hotel by annually paying the Bahamian government $100,000 with the provision that its records cannot be audited. In March, 1966, all three were indicted in New York for the

criminal need only to take a gambling casino's tourist boat or plane from Florida to Nassau, Bahamas (a 30-minute flight), walk without a passport through a customs station that imposes no limitation on the amount of money he carries, and go to a private bank on sober Bay Street that advertises "complete anonymity." The hoodlum uses any fictitious name that he chooses to deposit the money in a private bank, which then transfers the money to a commercial bank. Subsequently the commercial bank wires a draft in the private bank's name to the legendarily secretive Swiss banks.

Once unreported income reaches Zurich, Switzerland, Internal Revenue men concede, it is beyond legal reach. Cosmopolitan Switzerland's five *grossbanken* (great banks) and 4,200 bank offices epitomize solvency (the Swiss franc is backed by 120 percent gold) and cloak-and-dagger protection. To assure secrecy, Swiss banks will assign a new savings account depositor (who is charged instead of being paid interest) a six-digit numbered account that is known only to two or three senior bank officials. The depositor furnishes a handwriting sample by writing the account number in longhand, and is shown how to code any transactions. He can ask not to be sent any statements—which another government might confiscate as evidence of tax evasion—and need not worry about the *grossbanken* either confirming or denying that he has an account. Actually the Swiss Banking Act makes

---

third time for allegedly failing to pay $55,000 in wagering taxes when they reputedly ran a bookmaking operation in New York, from 1958 to 1964. In an earlier civil action, Internal Revenue attempted to levy $516,627 in wagering taxes against the three gamblers. But the Bahamian government doesn't recognize tax evasion as an extraditable crime and will not deport the gamblers.

providing any information about a depositor a criminal offense, punishable by six months in prison, a $5,000 fine and liability for any damages. And just how effectively the Swiss resist efforts to locate an account is told by one incident: When German Nazis tortured a depositor, the Swiss bankers shrewdly failed to locate an account for that person. Then when the victorious World War II allies obtained a court order demanding an accounting of the German deposits in Switzerland, the Germans received equal protection.

Hence an Internal Revenue agent's appearance at a *grossbanken* in pursuit of a tax evader doesn't receive much attention. Even when Internal Revenue obtained three separate court orders showing that an American undeniably evaded taxes (and thus the U.S. government had legal claim to his bank account), the Swiss refused to follow the order. If, moreover, the IRS agent had caught a tax evader going into the bank, he could receive no extradition cooperation. The Swiss government simply doesn't regard tax evasion as a crime. This secrecy tends to frustrate some IRS agents, but, as one has said, Swiss banks also can be a stimulus: "They're a reminder that you have to catch unreported income before it reaches Zurich."

Sometimes, however, IRS catches money being sent to Zurich *before* proving that it is unreported income. Such was the case of Antoine B. Rinieri, a French subject whom U.S. agents placed under surveillance when he flew from Paris to Chicago. On June 18, 1962, Rinieri boarded a Swissair plane flying from Chicago to Montreal to Zurich, but he did not reach either Montreal or Zurich. Agents from the U.S. Narcotics Bureau diverted the plane to New

York's Idlewild Airport, where they confiscated $247,500 in currency being carried by Rinieri on the assertion that it was profits from illicit narcotics sales. Then Internal Revenue took the money by levying a claim against Rinieri for $247,500 in "unpaid taxes." Insisting that he had taken the money to Chicago to buy art objects, Rinieri filed a suit to recover the $247,500 on grounds that he had not earned any money in the United States. On April 20, 1966, Federal Judge Richard H. Levet called Internal Revenue's actions "arbitrary, capricious and unconscionable" and ruled that the $247,500, plus 6 percent interest, be returned to Rinieri. Judge Levet added that the government had "not one iota of proof that any of this money was earned within the United States although approximately 46 months have passed . . . and this court has granted a two-month delay in proceedings in this matter in order to allow some 50 Treasury agents to attempt to trace the money."

If Internal Revenue's overseas personnel sometimes find their work hectic, they also can find refreshing consolation from observing other nations' tax collectors. Perhaps the most turbulent scene occurs annually in Italy. After wealthy Italians declare an estimate of their annual income, the tax agents investigate their bank accounts, income sources and living habits, then compile a "true" record of income that usually is 10 times higher than the person's estimate. But the tax collectors never mail the notice to the wealthy individual. Each December 26, the collectors post the list of incomes on a marble wall near Rome's Piazza della Bocca della Verita (Plaza of the Mouth of the Truth). On the list dated December 26,

1965, Count Goffredo Manfredi, a contractor, was first with a government-estimated income of 500 million lira ($823,600). Next came Prince Alessandro Torlonia, a property-owner, with an estimated income of 375 million lira ($602,000) and Sofia Scicolone (actress Sophia Loren) with an estimate of 350 million lira ($585,000). Manfredi's and Torlonia's personal estimates were about 10 percent of the government's figure, but Sophia Loren's calculation was evidently much lower. She hadn't even filed an estimate.

Elsewhere: West Berlin, which has twice as many men as women, offers tax concessions to German females who move there. Yet West Germany, which has the world's highest income tax rate, misses few sources: In 1966, it taxed a West German scientist on the $1,500 he received from slipping photostated documents to five Russian agents. In India, when females are told to appear for a tax audit, they frequently claim to be in *purdah,* a state of seclusion in which the woman covers her entire face and body and cannot be seen in public—let alone in a tax office! And in Brazil, taxpayers must, of all things, buy their income tax forms in stationery stores.

Collecting taxes on a global basis also is a reminder of the Internal Revenue Service's enormous size. Just one little-known division of IRS that imposes taxes on liquor and tobacco gathers more money each year than all taxes collected by any of 113 countries in the United Nations.

10

The Bottled-in-Bond Branch

Internal Revenue's 2,892-man Alcohol and Tobacco Tax Division (A&TT) functions so quietly that it is virtually unknown outside the trade. Yet, A&TT's role is so dominant that the liquor industry prefers that it remain unpublicized. Frankly, the Internal Revenue Service controls the nation's 355 legal distilleries. The purpose is to collect a heavy excise tax on the production of alcoholic beverages that is separate from the ensuing corporation tax on distillers' profits. In doing so, Internal Revenue's personnel have become the *only* persons allowed to open and close a distillery. In fact, Internal Revenue uses its own padlocks.

Moreover, in enforcing the Federal Alcohol Administration Act, Internal Revenue dictates a liquor's ingredients, basic formula, distillation, chemical content, aging, bottling, labeling and, sometimes, advertising. Thus, despite distilleries' myths and promotion about "time-honored formulas" and "master craftsmen," there is almost no difference in content (though tastes differ) between a fifth of a "premium" gin priced at $6.25 or a "medium-price" grade that retails for $4.79. Even the phrase "Bottled-in-Bond" appearing on labels to imply a distinctive quality simply means that Internal Revenue has permitted 100-proof whiskey held in "bonded" (dutiable) warehouses to be bottled before the excise tax was paid.

Federal excise taxes on liquor and tobacco have, of course, been levied intermittently since 1791. But the difficulties of collection were underscored by the Whiskey Tax Rebellion; and the 19th century Whiskey Rings of conspiring distillers, politicians and revenue agents who reported only fractions of the liquor produced. Consequently, Internal Revenue's Alcohol Tax Unit was given absolute authority over the liquor industry after Prohibition was repealed on December 5, 1933. The unit, consolidated into the Alcohol and Tobacco Tax Division in 1951, today produces nearly 5 percent of all federal revenues. In 1965, for example, A&TT collected $3,772,638,000 on alcoholic beverages and $2,148,594,000 from tobacco products—four times more taxes than Internal Revenue collected from the entire nation in 1933.

Louisville, where Kentucky's tobacco and bourbon belts meet, has a typical Alcohol and Tobacco Tax Division. Consisting of Permissive and Enforcement branches, it is part of the IRS District Office in Louisville's downtown Federal Building. But most of its employees are seldom seen there. The permissive branch's inspectors—men (and occasionally women) who have passed Civil Service tests and completed classroom instruction and on-the-job training—work mostly at the 17 nearby cigarette plants and breweries. They need not remain at the plants to determine tax liabilities. Internal Revenue has so regimented its system of cross-checking raw materials and final outputs that it needs only frequent spot checks (30,552 were made nationwide in 1965) to regulated breweries, wineries, alcohol plants and tobacco processors. "Hell their system is so pat that you can't hardly take a tax-free puff or sip of beer," laughs a vice president of a cigarette factory in Louisville's West End.

But Internal Revenue's "on-premise inspectors," whom the Service formerly named "storekeeper gaugers" and whom distillery employees call "G-men," almost never leave a legal distillery. Take, for example, the three on-premise inspectors assigned to National Distillers' Hill and Hill plant, a cluster of 17 red brick buildings. Each morning the three men drive directly to Internal Revenue's small brick building *at* National Distillery (IRS maintains comparable offices at 354 other distilleries), then unlock the bins containing raw ingredients. While 26 IRS employees once worked at National Distillery, the reduced supervision does not mean that the distillery is approaching the honor system. Internal Revenue holds (1) National's $10,320,000 bond, (2) the only keys to every bin, pipe and door in the distillery, (3) sensitive measuring equipment, and (4) right of confiscation. In short, these inspectors can nationalize the distillery *if* they find anything wrong.

Therefore nothing occurs during any major production of bourbon whiskey without Internal Revenue's supervision. Even incoming grain that is carried by conveyors to storage bins is weighed by IRS inspectors to calculate how much alcohol can be distilled from a shipment. Then, after the grain is cleaned and crushed into meal, the inspectors sample each mixture to ascertain that the bourbon is not made from less than 51 percent corn.° At subsequent stages, IRS's scientific instruments provide the surveillance: The meal is dumped into huge copper kettles of water, boiled into a sugar mash, then fermented by an addition of pure cultured yeast. This mash is pumped into enormous metal vats, called fermenters, that contain a portion of the previous day's mash to maintain continuity. For the next four days, the mash bubbles like a small, yellowish-born volcano, transforms into a soupy alcoholic mash called "beer," then is piped into copper tubes and distilled. Since alcohol boils at 173.3 degrees Fahrenheit—38.7 degrees lower than water—the whiskey separates and vaporizes into pipes leading through a condenser and into a "try" box. The name originates from the fact that the alcohol now is on "trial" with Internal Revenue and the master distiller, bourbon's equivalent of a chef. IRS inspectors read a complex hydrometer, compare figures and analyze samples to determine that the content does not exceed 160 proof or 80 percent alcohol.†

If both Internal Revenue and the distiller approve—and the process is so scientific that both invariably do—the alcohol enters a straining dubber, is redistilled and pumped into 40,000-gallon cisterns. Now one inspector reads meters that weigh the liquor to the .000006 percent of a pound. Another records how much rough "heads" and "tails" whiskey on the top and bottom of the cistern is removed. After distillation, the good whiskey is raw,

° Like most first-class bourbon distilleries, National makes its Hill and Hill bourbon (plus its Old Grand-Dad, Old Taylor, and Old Crow) from "secret recipes" of about 73 percent corn, 15 percent rye and 12 percent moistened barley malt that has sprouted about six inches.

† Pure alcohol would be called 200 proof.

colorless, 120-proof "white dog" that is diluted with distilled water to about 86 proof. Then it is drawn into new 55-gallon white oak barrels that have been completely charred inside and weighed empty (90 pounds) and full (480 pounds) by IRS inspectors. Only whiskey stored in such barrels for more than two years, Internal Revenue states, may be called "Bourbon," for this reason: As whiskey filters into a red layer of caramelized, charred oak, its color turns straw yellow after six months, becomes golden mahogany in two years and mellows at 3¾ to 8 years.

Internal Revenue's storekeeper gaugers, as the older name implies, keep the bourbon in storage. They watch as the barrels are stacked on open racks in one of 14 seven-story brick warehouses steam heated to 72 degrees because Internal Revenue also maintains—and National agrees—that whiskey seldom ages below 35 degrees. (Dissenting distillers who substitute what they call "good old mother nature's cold winters" for heated warehouses must note on Internal Revenue's red or green whiskey stamps that the bourbon is bottled in "spring" or "fall.") Then Internal Revenue's padlock is snapped, thereby "bonding" the warehouse. No premature removals are allowed except when chemists get IRS permission to periodically extract samples from every 50th barrel. These are the only tax-free "samples" that Internal Revenue allows and, ironically, National's own policy requires taste testers to spit out every shot they evaluate for maturity. "Now I'm strongly suspicious that some of this accidentally trickles down tasters' throats and they only motion toward the spittoon," jests J. E. "Chappie" Bland, National's red-faced, dapper resident manager. "More suspicious when some dedicated tasters finish about 10 samples and repeat the test to reassure themselves. Then their spittoon's drier'n a bone. Course, there's accidents. Fellows always choking and has a buddy pat him on the back."

Internal Revenue's rigid measurements prevent similar "accidents" elsewhere and render unnecessary such warning signs throughout the distillery: "IS A DRINK WORTH YOUR JOB?" There is, you see, little opportunity for the night shift to siphon off a quart milk bottle of sippin' whiskey. After aged bourbon is analyzed by both Internal Revenue and National chemists, it is poured into charcoal-filtered troughs leading to a metered bottling tank. Bottling, however, does not start until the distillery buys Internal Revenue's excise tax stamps used to seal bottles. This tax, $10.50 per proof gallon, is 10 times higher than liquor's production cost. The tax also is so closely computed that Internal Revenue inspectors can allow maximum tax-exempt "heels"—whiskey lost by evaporation or broken bottles—of only $\frac{1}{200}$ of 1 percent.[*]

Such taxes, therefore, prohibit National and many other distilleries from keeping an inventory of bottled whiskey. While distillers do delay federal taxes by bottling when orders are received, they often must borrow to pay excise taxes. National's 1964 debt, mostly for taxes, was $163 million. "Why you need a belt of bourbon to hear what we pay in excise taxes," Ben Corrado, a National executive, said one day at his office. Behind him hung a sign seen in most distillers' offices: "Nature of Business: WE COLLECT TAXES. Sideline: WE MAKE WHISKEY." Corrado pulled out a manila folder and read: "Taxes average

---

[*] This method is considered by some distillers as a major tax concession. Until 1960, Internal Revenue weighed incoming grain and collected the excise on the amount of liquor the grain was expected to yield.

one and a quarter million dollars every working day. It totaled $273 million in 1964. The county taxes us another $1.1 million. Then corporation taxes came to, let's see how many millions. . . ."

Distilleries have been the nation's most heavily taxed industry for continuing reasons. First, a theory prevails that someone who drinks a bottle of liquor each week will buy it regardless of price. Secondly, he will do minimal grumbling when the tax is levied during production and therefore avoids buying a bottle with a price tag that reads: "Cost: $2.25. Tax: $3.19. Total: $5.44." Third, large taxes on liquor suggest that the motive is rectitude, not revenue, and pleases Prohibitionists. The impression is especially prevalent in Kentucky, which produces 71 percent of the world's bourbon but forbids any liquor to be legally sold in 86 of 120 counties. For example, four of five women contacted one day in Elizabethtown, Kentucky, felt that high taxes on liquor were punitive measures to discourage the unmistakably evil beverage.

High excise taxes—plus state taxes that now average $1.96 a proof gallon—have discouraged some people from drinking *tax-paid* liquor. There is, to be certain, an alternative. A low-income man can enter a liquor store and buy a fifth (four-fifths of a quart) of whiskey that contains the Internal Revenue seal and costs $5.44. Or he can buy a quart fruit jar of untaxed moonshine whiskey for $2.25 from a bootlegger who hides it under an automobile seat. Often he buys moonshine. And if most individuals bought from moonshiners—anyone who makes whiskey without paying federal taxes—Internal Revenue's alcohol tax collections would diminish.

Enough moonshine whiskey is distilled to reduce alcohol taxes by at least 35 percent. The reason why most of the liquor is not sold is due to the tenacity of the Alcohol and Tobacco Tax Division's enforcement branch. These Internal Revenue investigators, better known as "revenooers" to moonshiners, are still fighting a guerrilla war against liquor tax evaders that astonishingly has continued since the Civil War. In 1965 alone, Internal Revenue's investigators arrested 7,171 moonshiners, destroyed 7,432 stills and 3,744,425 gallons of mash and liquor, and confiscated equipment, mostly vehicles used to transport liquor, valued at $2,486,193.

Such arrests often involve man-to-man combat between two tough, individualistic opponents. One is exemplified by "Fuzzy" Ander, a scrawny man who, acquaintances say appreciatively, had made "some of the best damn 'shine whiskey in Kentucky." The other by men such as William "Big Six" Henderson, an intense, 6-foot-2-inch, 230-pound IRS investigator with a left arm partially disabled by a moonshiner's 12-gauge shotgun blast. Henderson works about half of the week at a desk in Internal Revenue's district office in Louisville. During the remainder of the week, he usually changes into khaki clothing and boots, loads his .38 and .44 caliber revolvers, and drives into wooded areas looking for men like Fuzzy.

Fuzzy, meanwhile, does not make himself easily available during working hours. He also has had what he considered the two best means of deterring revenooers: He could run like a deer and he worked only at night. No Internal Revenue agent, Fuzzy was sure, would tramp three miles in the dark, through thickets cluttered with steep ravines and copperheads, to invade his hideout in a

173

wooded hollow between Poe Ridge and Pea Ridge, Kentucky. So one night Fuzzy lit a fire under his 55-gallon still. "Man," Fuzzy said, fondling a Mason jar of moonshine while his two teenage partners bottled the liquor, "wouldn't ol' Big Six Henderson just die if he was here right now? Let's have a little drink of white lightning to ol' Big Six." But ol' "Big Six" was there. He had covered himself with leaves and hid in a gully since before dark. Suddenly he reached out and grabbed Fuzzy's overalls. "Big Six, you rascal you!" Fuzzy said, more shocked at Henderson's ingenuity than angered. "Ah declare, man just can't make a decent livin' around you." When the two young associates ran, Big Six yelled, "Hey boys, I know your daddy. Ain't no use runnin'. We'll get you tomorrow." The boys stopped and came back. Then, after Henderson took a quart of moonshine for evidence and dynamited the still, everyone proceeded amiably to the U.S. Commissioner's office in nearby Bowling Green for the arraignment.

The case also illustrates why 96.7 percent of today's known moonshine is made in 14 southeastern states. In such rocky, hill-and-hollow areas comparable to where Fuzzy lives, most people can't afford (or in dry counties can't buy) tax-paid liquor and provide a ready market for moonshine. And moonshine techniques are not only passed down as an "honest trade," but with red clay land enabling most men to grow only a few corn nubbins and a hog, "shining" is regarded as the most sensible occupation. Entire families help operate the still, as evidenced by the variety of violators Internal Revenue investigators have caught: 10-year-old girls pouring moonshine into jars; 11-year-old boys (including one in business for himself) mixing the mash; "pregnant" wives carrying moonshine in automobile inner tubes worn around their waists; a 60-year-old grandmother who turned her hound dog on the revenooers; a spry 92-year-old Tennessean who supervised a large still; and a feeble 87-year-old moonshiner from Arkansas who had to be carried to a Federal Building (but not prosecuted when an A&TT supervisor reasoned that no judge would try him).

Hence, the South's hardened professional bootleggers, who operate 1,000-gallon stills and haul moonshine to large cities, can easily employ helpers resembling quaint grandchildren of Snuffy Smith, the comic-strip moonshiner. Or they hire Negroes who find working at a still offers free liquor, better pay and less drudgery than setting tobacco plants or picking cotton. Eventually many hired hands save up $50 and buy the materials to start their own "Jim Buck," "Alabama pot" or "ground hog" still—a process that simply involves digging a shallow hole to contain a fire around a pot or discarded oil drum. Then, instead of using any corn, most of these moonshiners boil sugar until alcohol vaporizes into the "thump keg"—usually another barrel or an automobile radiator—and is piped into a third barrel. The raw alcohol is cut with creek water or fruit juice to about 65 proof, poured into jars, aged for an hour or so, and then sold as *moonshine, 'shine, sugar likker, mountain dew, white mule, moon, shinny, sugar head* and *white lightning*.

Much of today's white lightning, IRS investigators contend, is made by cynical men with little pride in their product. Moonshiners in North and South Carolina have, for example, fermented mash with decomposed hog, chicken, opossum and snake carcasses, infested cow manure, then added Chlorox bleach, propane gas, or lye to give the booze an appearance of the desirable air bubble "bead." Other economical moonshiners who distill through cheap lead pipes and soldered radiators sometimes create poisonous moonshine. About 35 percent of the moonshine samples analyzed in Internal Revenue's National Office laboratory contain odorless, dissolved lead salts that collect in the brain until reaching the lethal proportions of .0004 of an ounce—a speck about the size of a pinhead. The eventual reaction has been spasms, blindness, paralysis, and death. Once IRS investigators watching a moonshiner in Tazewell, Tennessee, suspected of producing "bad stuff," knew that they had the right man: A purchaser took a long drink and collapsed 100 yards from the still.

No bad moonshine, though, ever equaled the 99-gallon batch concocted in Givinnet County, Georgia, by John R. (Fat) Hardy, a 360-pound convicted bootlegger. As does much of Georgia's 'shine, it filtered into south Atlanta's Negro "Peoplestown" section and was sold for 35 to 50 cents a drink in "crack joints," (kitchens) run by people called "Blind Pap" and "Big John." One Saturday night, it appeared that anybody in Peoplestown who took a drink soon screamed to get into Atlanta's Grady Memorial Hospital's emergency room. Fat Hardy's "likker," it turned out, contained only 5 percent moonshine, 34 percent methyl alcohol, and a little peach flavoring. It left 41 persons dead, 80 blinded or with impaired sight, and 300 violently ill. *

Another moonshine problem: Many local sheriffs and their deputies, who theoretically help IRS investigators

* Hardy was sentenced to life imprisonment for murder.

suppress untaxed liquor, are related or acquainted to moonshiners and alert them when "revenooers" are in town. Dozens of sheriffs are caught participating in moonshine operations each year, but few have surpassed the sheer brazenness of a county sheriff in South Carolina. According to testimony, the sheriff located stills, scared away the owners, sold the confiscated moonshine, then either consigned the still to another moonshiner or ran the business himself. He sold an estimated 20,000 gallons of 'shine over a five-year period before IRS investigators caught him in 1964. He was sentenced to four years in the penitentiary.

How, then, does Internal Revenue consistently pierce these local defenses? Since tactics vary in each state, the clearest picture comes from a briefing at the A&TT Division's Enforcement Branch in Washington. That branch chief until his retirement in September, 1965, was John Latham, a friendly, peppery little Louisianan whose knowledge of the South impelled the anti-moonshine drive.* And, just before his retirement, Latham piled his feet on a desk in his seventh-floor office and talked nearly four continuous hours.

"The No. 1 moonshining territory today," he began, "is under those big pine and oak trees in northeast Georgia. These violators get right onto the interstate highway and try to run tractor trailer loads of 'shine—big milk runs they say—out to Atlanta, Tennessee, Alabama, Asheville, North Carolina, right up to Washington, D.C. (a major outlet) and Brooklyn. Now the moonshiners had a head start on us. Hell, our office down in Georgia used to be so locally political that I couldn't have got a trainee's job

---

* Latham was succeeded by Tom Casey.

there. Thirty-four years as a government bum and they'd had the nerve to say I didn't have the experience. That's all cleaned out. Investigators we put there now come from everywhere else, California to Massachusetts, so local politics can't interfere. They're madder'n hell about it, too. Our boys had already arrested this one big moonshiner and then he lunges for a two-shot Derringer he's hidden and kills two of our men. They buried that violator with six pounds of lead in 'im.

"You got the figures that show how this work is as dangerous as coal mining?" Latham asked. Since the Alcohol Tax Unit was created in 1934, it was recalled, 30 investigators had been killed and 639 injured by gunfire, knifings, scalding, booby traps or automobile rundowns. "Add another number to that," Latham replied. "One of our finest boys was run down by a violator's car just yesterday. You have to get the jump on some of those hot-tempered (and sometimes intoxicated) moonshiners or you're gone. That's why we're not ashamed of our surreptitious gear. See, we got two quiet geniuses, Leo Paxton and Ray Seale, down the hall here who've developed over 100 pieces of electronic surveillance equipment. Like parabolic mikes that shoot down in a dark hollow and alert us if violators are working down there and saves sending a fine boy in there to get his head blown off in ambush. Doesn't that make sense? Then that Senator Long Committee's investigating how secret equipment is vi-o-lating people's privacy. He showed some government snooper scope that's supposed to help read license plates at 250 yards. We got one that can see for two miles."

Let Mr. Latham continue: "Another crucial thing our men have to do is stay one step ahead of those e-lusive 'shiners. Some'll operate all their life in some Godforsaken woods and then liable to turn up operating behind the police station. Take this one skinny hillbilly, no more than 130 pounds. He's following in his daddy's footsteps. Daddy's a big violator. Boy's only 27 years old and already spent about nine years in the penitentiary for making moonshine way back in some dismal woods that didn't even look explored. Two weeks after he gets out of the pen again and he's back in business. So New Year's Day, 1963, Jim West, one of our boys, pretends like he wants to buy some moon. Know where Jim catches this little peckerwood? He's rented him a 25-acre estate with a big split-level house right in the classy north-east section of Atlanta. Peacetree and Duniwoody Road. Has him a 1,500-gallon steel vat of moonshine inside. When our men mention getting a little publicity about the case in the Atlanta *Journal,* this peckerwood's eyes sparkle. He says: 'What about TV, too? OK? Hell fire, wait till I shave and change shirts.' So the moonshiner shaves and slicks down his hair and goes through the whole business of mixing the mash and bottling the stuff in front of the cameras."

No cameras, no audience, of course, watch a still being assembled. But they are located by four basic methods. The easiest, for Internal Revenue investigators, is using informers looking for a payoff ("$100'll do the trick") or revenge for getting some "real bad likker." "But hot-headed moonshiners make informing a damn precarious situation," emphasizes John Latham. "Two informers in Florida, for example, were found face down in a canal. Another'n found in a creek with a concrete block tied to him. Lots of informers are taken out in some dismal swamp or mountain ravine and never heard from again."

The second, and toughest method, is for Internal Revenue's undercover investigator to loaf in a little town in the moonshine belt pretending to be a bootlegger, moonshiner, alcoholic or seeking a job at a still. Look at how the stratagem worked on ol' Leroy, who hid his still in a depressing swamp beside the banks of Florida's Ochlockonee River. Each time Leroy entered a grocery, he saw the proprietor had displayed Internal Revenue Service's red, white and blue poster that read: "We don't sell sugar to MOONSHINERS. 100 pounds makes enough moonshine to defraud our government of $105.00 in taxes. We will not be the moonshiner's partner in crime."

Nevertheless, Leroy would calmly order a few cans of pork and beans, some Kerr Mason jars, then motion toward the stacks of Sucrest sugar and say, "Gimme five hundrit-pound sacks of sugar. Wife's doing some canning." But the storekeeper always said that Internal Revenue had asked him to limit sales to five percent of anyone's purchase. So Leroy mixed his moonshine mash out of sorghum molasses and Karo syrup. He kept adding yeast, but unaware that syrup contained preservative, couldn't ferment his mash. Finally, Leroy drove into town again seeking advice and luckily met a short, stocky hillbilly moonshiner who claimed he could ferment "any mash that ever was." "God bless your soul," Leroy grinned. "I'll pay you good." The new friends drove back to the still, but Leroy's moonshine buddy turned out to be IRS Investigator Jim West.

The third, and most productive method, is the standard "tip"—a white curl of smoke from a still—or a veteran investigator's intuition. Take the aforementioned "Big Six" Henderson, the Kentuckian who has arrested 5,200 moon-

shiners and bootleggers in his 25 years with Internal
Revenue. Once Clyde Webb, a county sheriff whom IRS
investigators trust, told Henderson about unverified reports of a stranger driving a large grocery truck loaded
with sugar toward Mammoth Cave, Kentucky. Big Six
recalled that this was the territory of two brothers—let's
call them the Peters boys—both previously convicted
moonshiners. He questioned grocers in the area, but their
answers provided no leads: "They ain't bought no sugar
since the last boy got out of the pen. Not even cookin'
sugar."

But Henderson knew the Peters boys' habits. He also
knew that they were capable of getting sugar from unscrupulous dealers. Thus, at 4 o'clock one morning Henderson and Webb drove toward the Peters' farm. The
area's intelligence system necessitated the early depar-
ture. Lookouts—usually sympathetic neighbors—often
use army surplus walkie-talkies. Unequipped lookouts,
whose voices echo for miles through windswept hollows,
sometimes yell the moonshiners' warning: "Fiah in the
hole!" Young "hunters" frequently fire shotguns at imaginary squirrels when they see a "revenooer." Or children
riding mules often dart past the raiders to alert their
moonshining relatives.

Two miles from the suspected site, Henderson drove his
automobile off the gravel road and hid it behind some
cedar trees. Webb erased the tire tracks with branches.
After moving through a woodland, the pair came upon a
barbed-wire fence that displayed a sign: "NO HUNTING
POSTED VILEATERS PROSCUTTED." "Hell, we know
what we're hunting for," Henderson drawled. Webb
laughed. About 5:15 the sun appeared and Henderson led

the way down a path ending at a wild blackberry patch and small creek. "You'll see these boys are no amateurs," Henderson whispered. "They could outproduce some of the distilleries with that setup." Underneath an army camouflage tarpaulin, leaves and blackberry bushes sat a 1,000-gallon copper still, six 800-gallon fermenters and 6,184 empty glass jugs. Two big watchdogs were tied to cedar trees.

Since Internal Revenue investigators must catch a moonshiner operating a still to obtain a conviction, the two men left. At 3 o'clock the next morning Henderson and Webb sneaked to a woodland overlooking the still and, when dawn came, watched the site through binoculars. They sneaked back eight consecutive nights until, finally, on the eighth morning, Henderson saw at least one hundred 100-pound bags of sugar had been carried into the area at night. "That means," he said, "they'll be mixing the mash tomorrow."

That night, Henderson and Webb formed an eight-man raiding squad that planned to surround the high ground around the still and, since the brothers usually hired someone to do the heavy work, wait until at least three men were present. "Now I'd like to handle this Curley," Henderson volunteered. "And he won't be hard to recognize." Curley, a type of man whom moonshiners call "an old meat and potatoes still hand," was clearly identifiable —his left ear had been bitten off in a fight. He also kept his low-cut shoes untied so that he could kick them off and run when he heard any revenooer approach.

The first 12 hours of waiting were tortuous. It rained almost continuously. Then, at 5 P.M., the sun finally came out. Minutes later the Peters boys appeared—not walking —but driving a Massie-Harris tractor hitched to a trailer they would use to transport their moonshine. Still the raiders waited until the third man sauntered up, and then, by prearrangement, simultaneously closed in. "Federal officers," Henderson said, his .38 revolver drawn. The announcement was only a formality. The Peters boys, veterans of surprise raids, recognized Henderson and re-acted as calmly as somebody receiving a restaurant check. Curley, as anticipated, ran. After a two-mile pursuit, Henderson, gasping for breath, caught Curley in a gully. When he returned to the still, which the agents were now preparing to dynamite, he found the older Peters brother beating a tree and repeating: "Son-of-a-bitch, son-of-a-bitch. . . ." Peters had realized that his new tractor-trailer, which cost $2,600, would be confiscated by the federal government.*

Internal Revenue's fourth technique is aerial surveil-lance. While small aircraft usually frighten rural moon-shiners away from their stills, they fly unnoticed over large cities where the remaining 3.3 percent of the moon-shine stills are seized: Detroit, Indianapolis, Brooklyn, New York, Philadelphia, Newark and Boston. Such metro-politan moonshiners are composed of two divergent classes. Detroit's moonshiners, for example, are indepen-dent operators who are called hillbillies, weedmonkies, pea pickers, poor white trash and poor black trash. Thus, periodically, a free-lance pilot who will be called Carl Rogers takes off at night in a single-engine Cessna from Detroit's Willow-Run Airport and circles above the Ham-track area on what Internal Revenue investigators call "U-2 flights."

---

* The tractor was sent to the Federal Penitentiary at Terre Haute, Indiana, for use on the prison farm. Ironically, the oldest Peters brother also ended up at the same penitentiary, where he told a guard that he once owned the tractor, was assigned the job of driving it.

The plane contains IRS's instrument that detects heat radiation and vaporizing alcohol from small stills hidden in the crowded low-rent apartment buildings. "The machine might pick up a laundry once in a while," Rogers has said, "but it doesn't miss many stills." He cannot afford to locate many laundries because he is paid only for each moonshine "hit." And when the machine makes a "hit," the pilot radios the location of the building to an Internal Revenue agent. At least two agents speed off in an unmarked black Ford that is equipped with a "whiffer" —a delicate instrument that detects the yeast smell of moonshine mash and thereby indicates the precise floor where the still sits. But IRS agents aren't allowed a slight margin of error. If they raid, say, apartment 4B, but the still is in 4C, this can bring repercussions from, say, the National Association for the Advancement of Colored People. So the undercover investigators—often Negroes if they are in a Negro area—enter the building carrying a smaller "whiffer" inside a lunch box. After pinpointing the still, investigators are under explicit orders to make the arrests and grab the evidence before a crowd angrily gathers outside. "And *grabbing* the evidence gets kind of complicated," maintains one veteran Internal Revenue officer. "The evidence is a red-hot still."

Similar scientific tactics strengthened Internal Revenue's drive, begun in 1958, against crime syndicates' moonshine operations in New York, Brooklyn, Newark and Boston. The syndicates' column-type stills, actually small distilleries complete with gauges and locks, often cost over $100,000 and require five specialized engineers to install them. They were detected in frame houses near Brooklyn's teeming Coney Island arcade, in warehouses, an old naval brig, and on barges floating off Long Island. One moonshiner in Brooklyn had such a large route that he insured against a seizure by Internal Revenue stopping his business. He brazenly kept an emergency still and Sucrest sugar stacked to the ceiling in an old city-owned silo in Queens, New York, directly across the East River from the United Nations building. Only the U-2 flights and "whiffer" had thought to look there.

Another seizure in Brooklyn, significantly, illustrates how the most ultrasensitive detection system ever developed by Internal Revenue—and possibly by the federal government—is deployed against moonshiners. When revenooers arrested two Georgia men driving a low-slung rented truck loaded with moonshine through Brooklyn, Internal Revenue wanted to implicate the moonshiner back in Georgia. Investigators in Atlanta went out to a nearby farmhouse where they felt the shine had been loaded and scooped up samples of red clay soil around the truck tire tracks, enabling Internal Revenue's scientists to prove in court in March, 1964, that the Georgia clay—and the clay particles underneath the truck seized in Brooklyn —could originate only from the same place and thus the Georgia moonshiner was guilty of a conspiracy. How? Scientists in Internal Revenue's one-room laboratory in the basement of the National Office in Washington have made a startling invention: an infallible neutron activation analysis (NAA) that uses atomic radiation to separate particles to one-billionth of a part and identify any substance more accurately than a fingerprint. That is the kind of planning Internal Revenue does to collect taxes or, hopefully, minimize the amount of taxes that eludes it.

11

The Non-tax Department

Item: Seventeen Americans who each had incomes exceeding one million dollars in 1963 did not pay any income tax.

Despite its awesome reputation and authority—and the fact that it does gather $119.7 billion a year—the Internal Revenue Service actually collects taxes on only 45 percent of all income in the United States. The remaining 55 percent: personal exemptions and deductions, adjusted incomes too small to be taxed, unreported entrepreneurial earnings, and income that is legally immune from all taxation. It is the latter tax-exempt income, representing about $61 billion a year or enough to lower everyone's taxes by about 30 percent, that provokes continuous clamoring by reformers to "close the loopholes" and "end tax inequities."

But is all income beyond Internal Revenue's jurisdiction an inequitable advantage? Consider, for instance, the aforementioned 17 Americans. They invested their money in state and municipal bonds, which pay a rate of interest lower than banks or U.S. Savings Bonds, but, by law, are tax-exempt income. The validity of whether such bonds' interest should be nontaxable may or may not be questionable today. Still the point is that the bonds, and resultant tax-free income, are available to anyone who can purchase them. As the late Justice Learned Hand aptly summarized, "There is nothing sinister in so arranging one's affairs as to keep taxes as low as possible . . . nobody owes any public duty to pay more than the law demands."

The genuine tax inequity is preferential treatment given individuals that exceeds all privileges available to anyone else: the proliferation of special taxation laws—laws that Internal Revenue must follow—that have created a *de facto* nontax department within IRS. The most debatable area is vividly shown when Internal Revenue's engineering and petroleum specialists audit oil companies' returns. An oilman is legally permitted to subtract the first 27.5 percent of his income for a "depletion allowance" before even starting to figure his taxes on the same terms as other businessmen or individuals. Such an advantage evolved from Internal Revenue's ruling in 1916 that allowed oilmen to deduct from taxable income the "fair market value," or cost, of drilling an oil well, much like businesses are permitted to gradually deduct depreciating equipment's cost. Then Congress, with persuasion from oil blocs, enacted a law setting a depletion allowance at 27.5 percent on the assumption that oil was a diminishing natural resource. Allowances varying from 23 to 5 percent have since been given producers of natural gas, ores, uranium, and coal.*

View, therefore, what can occur when an oilman strikes oil and grosses, say, $1,000,000. First he deducts 27.5 percent, or $275,000 as tax-free income, then he deducts all business expenses such as geological exploration and labor. Instead of paying taxes on the balance, many oilmen, to use their expressions, "drill up the rest" by "wildcatting" or boring more holes. If they strike a large oil stream, they pyramid their wealth. If they drill a dry hole, they lose little. The inequity simply is that other speculative businesses cannot take a depletion allowance. This privilege enables giant oil corporations to pay an average of only 23.6 percent taxes on their income while comparable corporations pay 47.7 percent. The unfairness appeared even more obvious when Internal Revenue studied 27 oil companies' returns over a 10-year period. While the companies' annual income ranged from $134,000 to $2,200,000 a year, one of the companies paid *no* taxes for 7 of the 10 years, another didn't pay any taxes for 5 years, one didn't pay for 4 years, and 4 others paid no taxes for 10 years. Another oilman, whose *net* income averaged from $5 million to $14 million dollars, paid only six-tenths of 1 per cent in taxes.

Two factors nullify a few Congressmen's attempts to reduce the oil depletion allowance. First, the petroleum

* Although Internal Revenue's regulations do not mention water as a tax-deductible diminishing natural resource, one farmer succeeded in deducting it. Marvin Shurbet, a wheat and cotton farmer on Texas's southern High Plains, deducted $377.91 on his 1959 return for water used to irrigate his crops. When IRS disallowed the deduction, Shurbet took his case to Texas District Court and won. Internal Revenue appealed to New Orleans' Fifth Circuit Court of Appeals, but, in 1965, Shurbet's claim was upheld.

lobby is perhaps the best-financed in Washington, exerting paralyzing pressures by campaigning against any Congressman who opposes their interest. Secondly, powerful Congressional leaders have traditionally favored the oil bloc. Texas' late Sam Rayburn, Speaker of the House for 17 years, and then-Senate Majority Leader Lyndon Johnson have staunchly defended the allowance. None, though, were as blatant as Oklahoma's late Democratic Senator Robert S. Kerr, multimillionaire oil and gas producer (whose oil firm didn't pay *any* tax one year), chairman of Kerr-McGee Industries, and ranking member of the Senate Finance Committee, which analyzes, then kills or passes all tax legislation. "Not vote or campaign for keeping the oil depletion allowance?" Kerr would roar. "Now wouldn't that be a helluva thing if the U-nited States Senator from Oklahoma didn't look out for his own people? Helluva thing."

A second privilege is to devise a special tax law for one person. Such a recipient was a contractor from Oklahoma City who found himself in income tax difficulties in 1955–56. After receiving $995,000 from the government in 1949 as a final payment for wartime construction, the contractor first failed to declare the money, then after Internal Revenue began investigating him, declared it as a capital gains transaction, which would have been taxed at a 25 percent rate instead of the then-maximum rate of 91 percent. In 1955, Internal Revenue sued the contractor for $729,446 in taxes and $226,258 in interest and penalties. The Tax Court not only upheld the IRS position, but criticized the man for filing blank income tax returns for three years. The Supreme Court refused to review his appeal, leaving no legal choice but to pay the $955,704.

Two months later, Senator Kerr attached a precisely worded amendment called "Certain Claims Against the United States" to the bottom of an obscure bill leaving the Finance Committee. Unnoticed and undebated, the amendment became Public Law 84-269,70, Statute 40, which made it *illegal* to charge the contractor more than 33 percent taxes or *any* interest and penalties. Thus he was relieved of paying at least $650,000 in taxes and penalties.

Sometimes the special bill need not even be passed. Consider the maneuvers of Representative John W. Byrnes of Wisconsin, first-ranking Republican on the House Ways and Means Committee, which drafts all tax legislation. In 1959, Byrnes was contacted by an acquaintance from Milwaukee, Paul J. Rogan, an official of Mortgage Guarantee Insurance Company—MAGIC as the company was called—about a tax problem. Wisconsin laws compelled MAGIC to keep a reserve account for 15 years and Internal Revenue taxed the profits, much as it taxes an individual's interest from savings accounts. Twice Internal Revenue had refused MAGIC's request to end the tax. Unfair? Evidently Byrnes thought so. He began to telephone and write letters on MAGIC's behalf to both the Secretary of the Treasury and Internal Revenue. When these moves failed to persuade Internal Revenue to change the ruling, Byrnes introduced legislation to eliminate taxes on earnings from MAGIC's reserve funds. Whereupon Internal Revenue reversed its position on MAGIC on the theory that it would rather allow one quiet concession than to see a law enacted forcing it to grant exceptions to hundreds of other companies.

The fact might not have been disclosed except for one

development. Six months later Byrnes was allowed to invest $2,300 in MAGIC stock at prices *below* the market value (or "exercising a stock option" according to the official jargon). Three years later the stock's value was nearly $23,000! Then, since another of MAGIC's stockholders turned out to be Bobby Baker, the former Senate majority secretary whose unusual financial affairs began to be divulged in 1963–64, Byrnes' ownership in MAGIC was simultaneously revealed. Quickly Byrnes rushed to the House floor to deny he had committed any indiscretion. In tears, he announced that he would sell his MAGIC stock and give all profits to a scholarship fund, then adding: "I didn't do anything in this case that any other congressman wouldn't do for a constituent or a business in his state that had a tax problem."

The statement left an important question: Just how many intricate laws are deliberately or inadvertently eased through to reduce certain individuals' or companies' tax liability? The cases appear endless. In an earlier but classic example, Louis B. Mayer, former president of Metro-Goldwyn-Mayer movie studio, was able to angle his own Section No. 1240 in an Internal Revenue Amendment that allowed his termination profits of $5 million from M.G.M. to be taxed at the capital gain's rate of 25 percent instead of the then-maximum 91 percent on income above $200,000. His savings? At least $2 million.

To comprehend how special nontax laws are enacted— as well as the major tax legislation responsible for Internal Revenue's existence—it is necessary to know our tax structure. All tax bills must, as the U.S. Constitution states, originate in the House of Representatives. That doesn't mean, of course, that only U.S. Representatives can conceive legislation on taxes. When President Johnson sought to reinstate the previously reduced excise taxes on telephone calls and sales of automobiles in 1966, his Secretary of the Treasury (or assistant secretary in smaller matters) makes such a proposal to the House Ways and Means Committee. The committee, composed of 25 congressmen and headed by Wilbur Mills of Arkansas, sits at a horseshoe-shaped mahogany table in an imposing hearing room decorated with a chandelier and oil paintings of the committee's former chairmen. First, Mills, then other representatives in order of seniority, question the Treasury's spokesman to more or less establish the necessity of such legislation. But the committee's anonymous staff of 19 lawyers and tax specialists take the Treasury's "suggested drafts" and write all tax legislation. Most voluminous bills, usually given only superficial reading by the congressmen, are seldom questioned.

If the bill passes the Ways and Means Committee, then a majority of the House, it goes to the 17-member Senate Finance Committee, which is chaired by Louisiana's Senator Russell B. Long.* A major bill faces much the same treatment in the Finance Committee, except that its smaller staff (eight employees) also receives technical recommendations from 25 tax specialists on the Congress's Joint Committee on Internal Revenue Taxation. When the House's bill—often amended or slightly rephrased—is

* Long's position to exert control over Internal Revenue's legislation represents an irony. On Friday, September 6, 1935, Internal Revenue's Intelligence Division concluded a four-year investigation and evidence of alleged tax evasion that its agents said would help convict Chairman Long's father, Huey (Kingfish) Long, a demagogic governor and then U. S. Senator from Louisiana, on other federal charges. No indictment ever resulted. On Sunday night, September 8, Huey Long was mysteriously killed—purportedly by a gunshot fired into the abdomen—in a corridor of Louisiana's Capitol.

passed by the Finance Committee and the Senate, it is debated (sometimes sparingly) in a House-Senate committee, then repassed by the House and sent to the President for his signature. Ostensibly the system has deterrents against any special laws except for what is called "Congressional courtesy." Each Congressman can, if he wishes, sponsor one or two private bills per session without being questioned. Though senators cannot write tax bills, they may add any unrelated amendment whatsoever to a bill.

The opportunity to manipulate tax laws, even by outsiders and without Congressmen's knowledge, was bluntly pointed out by Representative Wright Patman, a 73-year-old, self-styled fiscal crusader, when he rose on the House floor on March 30, 1965, and said:

In the last Congress, major tax legislation was enacted. Every American and every business, large and small, was affected one way or another by this legislation. Hearings on the tax legislation ran into seven volumes covering 4,000 printed pages. What a splendid opportunity for shenanigans. I wonder how many of my colleagues read the 4,000 pages. Who really knows what that legislation was all about unless they read it? How many cases of petty and grand larceny are involved? Who really knows the answers to these questions?

I am not in any way criticizing the extremely able gentleman who is chairman of the Ways and Means Committee that handles tax matters or any member of that committee. I merely state that they—as I am—are forced to rely too often upon information from lobbyists who have axes to grind, and it is physically impossible for the members of the committee or the Congress to know whether or not there are sleepers in some of these "Whereases" and the "Therefore be it enacteds" that infect our legislation.

On top of this, Internal Revenue increases the mystique about most tax rulings. How? First, Congress's periodic tax laws and amendments, when added to the Internal Revenue Code, now total more than 20,000 pages about the size of 16 cumbersome Sears, Roebuck catalogues. Then the incredibly complex language, often written in generalities and 600-word sentences, must be translated by Internal Revenue into specific rulings. Yet Internal Revenue publishes only 340 of its 34,000 annual technical rulings on whether or not a situation—both actual and hypothetical—qualifies for a certain tax status. Indeed, considerable merit exists for Internal Revenue's reasoning: Only rulings with broad applicability need be made public. But Internal Revenue's staunch refusal to release any other rulings creates a secretive atmosphere suggesting (though it may be entirely baseless) that many rulings allow generous favoritism in special situations.

A case in point developed in 1965 when the Senate Finance Committee held a closed meeting to debate how the giant E. I. DuPont de Nemours & Co. of Wilmington, Delaware, had obtained a ruling from Internal Revenue—which reversed IRS's previous position on the same matter—that secretly relieved it of at least $56 million and possibly $100 million in taxes. The private ruling grew out of the Supreme Court's decision in 1961 that DuPont, in accordance with antitrust laws, sell its 23 percent ownership in General Motors to avoid the "reasonable probability" that it might someday be in a position to monopolize G.M.'s purchases. At that time, Congress passed legislation specifically allowing DuPont to pay only the 25 percent capital gains tax rate on profits from the divestiture.

Then in 1964, DuPont's attorney, Clark Clifford, in pointing out that the value of its General Motors' stock had risen and therefore increased IRS's tax receipts on the sale to about $612 million, evidently obtained this private ruling on Public Law 87-403: Some of DuPont's stock, when transferred from Christiana Securities Co., the Du-Pont-controlled holding company, to some of DuPont's tax exempt foundations, would not be taxed at all. While Internal Revenue's decision may have been its only legal alternative, as Kentucky's Senator Thruston Morton pointed out, circumstantial evidence implied a different picture: (1) DuPont's attorney in the negotiations was a former member of President Truman's White House staff and an advisor to President Johnson. (2). After DuPont's ruling was disclosed, then-Secretary of the Treasury Douglas Dillon refused to discuss why the ruling was reversed.

The champion technique of tax avoidance is strikingly evident in the small section of most Internal Revenue District offices called Exempt Organizations Branch. Typically, employees are busily putting paper clips on IRS Forms 1021 and 990-A, but, unlike IRS returns in other branches, no checks are attached. They never have been. They undoubtedly never will be. These returns are filed by nonprofit private foundations that are legally exempt from all federal taxation whatsoever.* Since foun-

* About 280,000 of an estimated 1,000,000 nonprofit organizations are required to file returns even though they pay no taxes. Besides foundations, they are civic and social welfare organizations, labor unions, social and recreational clubs, fraternal orders, business leagues, cemetery corporations, mutual organizations, pension funds and scientific, literary and religious organizations.

dations were virtually nonexistent before the advent of Internal Revenue, they must be regarded as subsisting primarily to avoid inheritance and income taxes. Pioneered by such ultrawealthy persons as Henry and Edsel Ford, John D. Rockefeller and Alfred I. DuPont as a means to channel money into charitable trust funds instead of paying estate taxes that would erode their financial empires, tax-exempt foundations have suddenly become common for all income classes. So common that foundations have fostered a semi-joke: A status seeker is no longer judged by the number of automobiles he owns, but by the number of foundations he controls. Today there are even, to name just three, a Prairie Chicken Foundation of Illinois that works to "preserve" the remaining prairie chickens; the Lollipop Foundation of America that one day each year gives 300,000 suckers to hospitalized children; and *Playboy* magazine's Playboy Foundation that claims to have been "organized to pursue, perpetuate and protect the principles of freedom and democracy expounded in the Playboy Philosophy . . . (is) supported by contributions (that) are tax deductible."

In fact, nobody really knows how many tax-exempt foundations exist and how much they control. Says Internal Revenue's Director of Information, Joseph S. Rosapepe: "The word 'foundation' is not defined in the Revenue Code nor in the Regulations," but, accepting the definition in the Treasury's study, there "are approximately 15,000 to 20,000 such organizations." Others have catalogued at least 45,124 tax-exempt foundations and these are only organizations that the Treasury and Internal Revenue know exists. Almost daily, a tax-free foundation is found—or voluntarily admits—to have been in existence for 25 or 30 years without bothering even to apply for tax-exempt status or file a tax-exempt Form 990-A. While the exact amount of all foundations' total assets is equally vague, this much is known: Between 1962 and 1964, Representative Wright Patman, as chairman of a House Subcommittee on Small Business, investigated 534 of the larger tax-exempt foundations and found that despite what he called efforts "to confuse, confound, befuddle and bemuddle" they controlled at least $10.3 *billion* in tax-free assets. The magnitude of foundations was reflected when Internal Revenue, reacting to Patman's criticism to its administration of tax-exempt organizations, appointed a 14-man advisory committee to study the situation. Ten of the 14 men were affiliated with foundations.*

The opening to allow the diversion of money into foundations began innocuously. The Revenue Acts of 1909 and 1913 excluded from taxation the incomes of charitable or nonprofit organizations but limited the amount of contributions that could be deducted from taxable income. Then a wealthy nun inherited a large piece of property that she wanted to give to charity. Since the property's value exceeded the maximum tax-deductible donations, a law was enacted to allow virtually unlimited deductible gifts in certain situations. Charitable, nonprofit foundations, if engaged in impartial programs to improve educa-

* An equally high ratio of the Administration's top echelon shuttle between the government and foundations. John W. Gardner, the Secretary of Health, Education and Welfare, is on leave of absence as president (at an annual salary of $50,000) of the nonprofit Carnegie Corporation. Dean Rusk, the Secretary of State, previously served as president of the Rockefeller Foundation. McGeorge Bundy resigned as the White House's special assistant to become the Ford Foundation's president.

tion, health, science, literature, and the like, met these specifications.

Undoubtedly many of today's foundations do creditable work in line with the aim stated on the inside cover of the Ford Foundation's brochure: ". . . to advance human welfare." This is proven just by looking at the schools and libraries built by foundations.* Besides, some foundations probably can give away money just as equitably as the federal government. Nevertheless, thousands of self-serving foundation propagandists have built an image that every cent spent, every endeavor by a foundation is a noble act of philanthropy. The fact is, as reaffirmed by Representative Patman's audit, that most foundations are a fraud. Only about 50 percent of the tax-free income received by the foundations that Patman investigated was spent in the direction of charity. Too, several foundations spent as little as 7 percent for charitable pursuits; others didn't spend anything toward charity (except to close relatives).

Consider two typical abuses. A man established what shall be called a Deserving Student Scholarship Foundation, went through the formality of filling out an IRS Form 1023 and obtaining tax-exempt status, then donated $10,000 to the foundation. First, he paid no taxes on the $10,000 donation and dropped his taxable income into a lower rate of taxation. What's wrong with that noble act? Both of the Foundation's scholarships—or the $10,000— were awarded to the philanthropist's two children, who spent a total of about $4,300 for education and returned the balance to their father. In a second scheme, a busi-

---

* Foundations account for 8 percent of all private gifts in the United States.

nessman in New Jersey organized a tax-exempt foundation and donated $30,000 to its cause, then transferred the tax-free gift back to his corporation as a "loan" that he never intended to repay. Next the penniless foundation, drained of its funds by a "bad debt," declared bankruptcy.

Such techniques of funneling stock or money from corporations to tax-exempt foundations has become so prevalent that it has a trade name, Bootstrap Operations, and has gained an advantage over taxpaying small businessmen. "Nonprofit" foundations are quietly operating profitable businesses such as loan companies, real estate syndicates, commercial movie and television productions, restaurants, gas stations, house trailer parks, brokerage firms and promotion syndicates.

Too, foundations allow the accumulation of enormous wealth without paying any taxes. At least 111 of the 546 foundations investigated by Patman's subcommittee owned from 10 to *100 percent* of the stock in a total of 263 corporations, including such familiar names as Ford Motor Company, Great Atlantic and Pacific Tea Company (A & P), Eli Lilly & Co., Kellogg Company and S. S. Kresge. For example, the Rockefellers' seven foundations owned, at the time of the audit, 7,891,567 shares of common stock in Standard Oil of New Jersey that then had a market value of $324,946,110; 602,127 shares of stock worth $23,610,770 in Socony Mobil Oil Company, and 2,130,453 shares valued at $97,835,710 in four other oil tank companies. None of the stock's millions of dollars in earnings, unlike most other stockholders' dividends, is subject to taxes.

What can Internal Revenue do about foundations' abusing tax-exempt privileges? The Service has authority to act in situations that it calls "prohibited transactions" and "unreasonable accumulations." And when IRS finds that a foundation is not a genuinely nonpartisan educational or charitable corporation, it can recommend revocation of that foundation's tax-exempt status—which means donations to that organization are no longer tax deductible. But, as a leading IRS official conceded before Patman's subcommittee, the Service was "not exceedingly proud" of its record in examining foundations. Furthermore, then-Commissioner Mortimer Caplin's inability even to report about how many audits that IRS had made on the aforementioned 534 foundations, Patman emphasized, is what motivated his investigation.

Afterwards, Patman made an incisive criticism of Caplin's management: "Our findings show that the Internal Revenue Service record—in terms of supervision of foundations—is a dud, a dismal failure. Commissioner Caplin's performance has been no better than that of his predecessors. While the Commissioner deplores the lack of such supervision prior to 1961 and has released torrents of words during the past two years assuring the Congress and the public that the Internal Revenue Service is engaged in intensive examination of tax-exempt foundations, there is no recognizable sign of progress in this area. Signs are multiplying that the Internal Revenue Service cannot meet its responsibilities through ringing statements by Commissioner Caplin, press agentry, and public relations gimmickery; and [needs] fewer speeches by the Commissioner." Patman and his long-time assistant, Harry Olsher, had found enough cases to document the subcommittee's conclusions. In fact, they located tax-exempt foundations that Internal Revenue didn't know existed: Examples:

• The Parsons-Blewett Memorial Fund of St. Louis admitted that it was organized in 1916, but didn't even file an income tax return or application for tax-exempt status until 1959 because it had received no such requests from Internal Revenue until 1961 and "consequently none were filed."

• The Rutherford B. Hayes and Lucy W. Hayes Foundation of Spiegel Grove, Ohio, began functioning as a tax-exempt foundation in 1926, but didn't file its first 990-A tax return until 1961, or 35 years later.

• The Isaac W. Bernheim Foundation of Louisville, whose receipts over a five-year period totaled $1,205,108, started operating as a tax-exempt organization in 1930 but filed its first return in 1955. The group had been telephoning Internal Revenue for years, declared Robert Paul, the foundation's executive director, "and it was only after considerable difficulty I could find someone who could tell me in what manner this form should be made out to meet our particular situation."

There also seemed to be a reluctance even to contact the large eastern foundations. Examples:

• The 10 largest tax-exempt foundations (assets: $4.6 billion) in the group that Patman's subcommittee studied had not been audited by Internal Revenue.

• Eight of the nine foundations controlled by Ford and holding assets of $2,240,289,227 were not audited.

• Eleven of the 14 Rockefeller-controlled foundations, which had assets of $1,089,322,230, were not audited.

• None of the Carnegie Foundations' five tax-exempt groups, whose resources totaled $413 million, were audited.

- Six of DuPont's nine foundations, which held assets of $175.6 million, were not audited.
- Only 113 of the 546 foundations had been audited over a 10¾-year period and 98 of them had had only one audit during that period.

While Internal Revenue states that it audits about 12,000 (out of one million) tax-exempt organizations each year, it has reasons for such sparse supervision of foundations. First, the Service assigns audit manpower, explains Donald W. Bacon, IRS assistant commissioner for compliance, in order to "provide a high revenue yield per man hour of examination . . . under existing legislation, authorized tax-exempt status is not so frequently abused as to provide a fertile tax recovery field for the deployment of much of our relatively limited examining officer resources . . . We find some flagrant examples of abuse . . . and we find frequent technical deviations from procedural requirements or from operational commitments. These, however, are in many instances not sufficient to justify withdrawal of tax-exempt status."

Additionally, IRS emphasizes that its Exempt Organizations Branch has only 90 employees and is not equipped to scrutinize foundations' policies and ideologies. "Here we are confronted not only with the problem of numbers," says Bacon, "but also many knotty and complex conceptual problems of interpretation and semantics. What, for example, is meant by the words 'education' and 'religion' in relation to various ideologies as used in the statutes? Some of our most ticklish problems arise because we, as a tax administration organization, are expected to decide with the wisdom of Solomon, whether a 'religious' organization, or an 'educational' organization is so partisan that it may have sacrificed its tax exemption . . . Again, what is considered a 'little bit of business' for tax-exempt organizations competing with fully taxable businesses?"

The Service has made a few such decisions. In 1965, IRS revoked about 150 foundations' tax-exempt status, including that of Life Line Foundation, for "partisanship." There is little doubt that Life Line, largely supported by tax-deductible contributions from right-wing oilman H. L. Hunt, was a partisan educational foundation. Its broadcasters and pamphleteers crusaded against Communism and President Johnson during the 1964 Presidential campaign. Too, the procedure initiated what IRS labeled a "crackdown" on right-wing tax-exempt foundations. Yet IRS maneuvered itself into a position of where it is damned if it does, damned if it does not. Quickly, conservatives contended, no similar "crackdown" was directed toward left-wing educational foundations. Whether or not this is true, an inconsistency is apparent. IRS has, for instance, repeatedly denied a tax-exempt status for The Committee of One Million, which campaigns solely against the admission of Communist China to the United Nations, but allows tax exemption for the crypto-religious Fellowship of Reconciliation, which openly advocates Red China's acceptance into the U.N.

All in all, the Exempt Organizations Branch's lack of momentum—in contrast to zeal shown in collecting taxes and catching tax law offenders—is understandable. As a bureau judged primarily for the amount of taxes it collects, little enthusiasm can be expected from IRS for a job that produces only infinitesimal revenue.

12

The Internal Enemy

As part of their jobs, some employees in Internal Revenue's Manhattan District office frequently are driven five blocks across New York's lower east side to the huge, multicolumn marble United States Court House to recite evidence against individuals on trial for violations of tax laws. But for eight days during November and December of 1965, four former IRS auditors walked up steps from the IRT subway tunnel that opens onto the sidewalk between the Brooklyn Bridge's entrance and the U.S. Court. Then they testified for the government—not as a function of their employment but probably in anticipation of leniency if they were later prosecuted. All four had testified that between 1960 and 1965 they had accepted 13 payments totaling $550 from David B. Barash, a 46-year-old accountant-lawyer, while auditing some of his clients' tax returns.

And, as Barash's trial for alleged bribery began, the one-time IRS auditors described a disagreeable situation inside an Internal Revenue office: the "payoff." Just consider pertinent testimony from the first witness, Saul Wolf, who was employed in IRS's Audit Division for 21 years:

Q: Mr. Wolf, how was this particular return, referring to Government's Exhibit No. 6, assigned to you for audit?

A: I assigned it to myself.

Q: And when did this take place?

A: During lunchtime when I was acting supervisor.

Q: Prior to assigning this return to yourself, did you have a conversation with the defendant?

A: Yes I did. Two days before . . . the date of the audit. . . . He asked me to see if I could get the case assigned to myself and he would take care of me.

Q: And what did you respond when he asked you to assign the case?

A: I said I would.

Q: How did you go about assigning the case to yourself?

A: I just took it out of the drawer and assigned it to myself. I was acting supervisor, assistant. Mr. Sullivan, my supervisor, was out to lunch.

Q: How did you locate it?

A: Mr. Barash gave me the letter with the date on it and the name of the taxpayer. We got a file by date and taxpayers, alphabetical file.

Q: And is it normal procedure for an office auditor to assign an income tax return to himself?

A: No it isn't.

Q: And why in this instance did you depart from normal procedure?

A: Mr. Barash said there was something in it for me.

Q: And did you conduct an audit of entertainment expenses with respect to that particular return with Mr. Barash?

A: Well we didn't have much substantiation . . . I disallowed business expenses and entertainment expenses,

$433 and a medical adjustment of $9, total disallowance
of $442.

Q: And what did you allow in the way of business and entertainment expenses?

A: $3,032.

Q: Did you ask Mr. Barash in connection with your audit
of these travel and entertainment expenses whether the
substantiation which he did show was of business expenses as versus personal expenses?

A: No I didn't . . . Mr. Barash asked me to disallow an
amount and I did . . . I just gave him the waiver and
he told me to see him in a few days.

Q: Did you go see him in a few days?

A: Yes I did . . . I went to an office at 475 Fifth Avenue
. . . There were other people present, but Mr. Barash
took me into another room . . . He gave me $50 and I
thanked him.

After three other ex-auditors gave comparable accounts
of how they took $25 to $75 bribes from Barash, the latter
swore that the former IRS employees demanded the payments as part of a shakedown throughout Internal Revenue. Argued Barash's attorney: "Each was aware of the
thievery that existed in his respective group. They participated jointly in situations and believe me, we will show
you they advised each other how much to charge on a
case." Barash did admit giving the auditors "gifts" of $25
to $50 inside Christmas cards plus theater tickets and
lunches—after, he testified, one auditor allegedly said:
"You are going to have to wait a long time. I didn't get
paid on this return."

Then came Barash's version of the audit by Wolf.
Contending that he had not previously met Wolf and had
"arrived at a fair and agreeable figure of additional tax,"
Barash testified: "He entered into a conversation with me

at the tail end of the audit . . . His remarks were that he heard about me through the grapevine and he heard that I was not one of the givers, per se."

Q: Yes?
A: However, he felt, or he expressed himself that he was doing something—I don't know what it was that he was doing, but he said he was doing something and because of that he wanted something.
Q: For what reason?
A: He said that he was bending backwards to give me a break on this audit. As far as I was concerned, there was no break. I had a proper audit. I had a fair set of figures. He gave me or disallowed a sum of $442 out of a nominal sum of expenses which I had substantiated. He wasn't doing anything for me. He had—He made big issue about it. It was just about that time that, coincidentally, I had a pair of theater tickets that were given to me by a client for a show, a Broadway show . . . I asked him if it would be—if he would like to have these tickets, and he says—he was happy. He would like to, he would like it very much.

Barash was convicted of bribery, but on August 3, 1966, the Court of Appeals reversed the conviction and ordered a new trial.

Two important questions about Internal Revenue's inner workings arise in cases where convictions of bribery have been sustained: How much and how often do accountants, lawyers and taxpayers illegally offer or pay money to Internal Revenue's employees to compromise a decision? How many IRS employees demand payment from taxpayers or their representatives? Incomplete answers emerged, in disconcerting frequency, at the same U.S. Court House between 1961 and 1966 as over 225 individuals—about equally divided between (a) employees and former employees in Internal Revenue's Manhattan and Brooklyn District offices and (b) accountants, lawyers and taxpayers—were indicted, convicted or pleaded guilty to collusion, extortion or bribery involving fraudulent tax returns.

Such fraud *by* tax collectors is not, of course, new. Internal Revenue has been intermittently plagued by theft by its own employees since, weeks after its inception, dozens of wholesome-looking collectors who traveled by horseback to gather income taxes kept riding west. While today there is a lower ratio of internal fraud per employee, the problem is much more insidious, much harder to detect than, say, bank employees who distort records to steal. Unlike banks that deal in certain amounts of currency and know that most embezzlement eventually will be detected by competent outside auditors, Internal Revenue has no built-in deterrent. IRS investigators, agents and auditors deal in discretionary areas and often can decide whether evidence warrants possible prosecution or whether someone owes $3,000 or $30 for taxes. Accordingly, when a IRS employee takes $300 in cash to ascertain that incriminating evidence goes unreported or the amount of taxes due is closer to $30, there is no discrepancy on record for independent auditors to find.

The absence of this automatic system of checks and balances makes it illogical to assume that all fraud within IRS is discovered. In fact, how the aforementioned 225 cases were discovered—and the corruption's long-term pattern and magnitude—suggests that some fraud by employees escapes detection. The investigation began only after rumors circulated and taxpayers in New York complained that they had to give accountants "payola money" for IRS auditors.* When some guilty IRS employees were questioned, they implicated certain accountants and lawyers. The latter, in turn, identified current or former IRS personnel involved in tax fixes. Subsequently, Internal Revenue's Inspection Division (IRS's intra-investigative branch that is described later) centralized and ferreted out evidence of fraud in, predominantly, the audit divisions and among collection officers and supervisors paid up to $17,500 a year. Yet, as an example of how long the fraud went unnoticed, investigators found a businessman who admitted giving an agent $25,000 during audit, but the agent couldn't be prosecuted because the five-year statue of limitation had expired. This situation was true in many other cases.

According to government prosecutors, such situations as these were common in Internal Revenue's Manhattan and Brooklyn District offices:

1. A 59-year-old tax technician passed up opportunity for promotion in order to remain in a lower-paying position in which he allegedly received $15,000 to $25,000 a year in bribes to "look the other way" when reviewing returns of one tax practitioner's clients who are well-known in theatrical and boxing circles.

2. Dozens of employees in the audit divisions, many working up to 30 years at IRS, accepted or extracted bribes ranging from $50 to $250. Others took up to $2,000, and occasionally $20,000 per case, from accountants and lawyers to close cases of individuals who had important positions or shady backgrounds; destroy records that

---

* Taxpayers should know, too, that some accountants falsely insinuate that they "had to take care of the Internal Revenue man" in order to charge exorbitant fees.

showed certain taxpayers owed a substantial amount in taxes, or assure accountants that their clients' returns would not be audited.

3. A tax-fixing ring allegedly organized by a junior high school remedial-reading teacher and a revenue agent in Internal Revenue's Manhattan District Collection Division operated for three years before arousing suspicion. As a federal grand jury indictment charged, the agent initially paid approximately $5,000 to four other IRS employees to process fraudulent returns. Then the ring grew to include at least 19 relatives and acquaintances of the conspirators, and 8 IRS employees who took about $225,000 in bribes to accept 2,419 tax returns that had falsified exemptions and deductions, understated salaries earned and raised amounts of taxes withheld by employers. This scheme enabled the ring to receive more than $1.5 million in phony refunds. Only about 25 to 40 percent of the refunds went to participating "taxpayers."

Unprecedented boldness led to the scheme's exposure. During the probe, IRS investigators found 35 returns with unusual characteristics: Returns filed by residents of Brooklyn and Queens, New York, had been sent—not to the Brooklyn IRS office but the Manhattan office—and summarily accepted by the eight IRS employees! Dozens of doctors' and dentists' returns had identical handwriting and deductions. Returns with Christian names listed large contributions to Jewish synagogues and taxpayers with Jewish names purportedly donated heavily to churches. Other individuals listed large and different numbers of children from year to year, and, in most instances, claimed each child needed special safety shoes that qualified as medical deductions. Even many secretaries' returns showed deductions for "hazardous work shoes" normally worn by ironworkers.

Internal corruption naturally is not limited to IRS's Manhattan and Brooklyn offices. During the same period between 1961 and 1966 about 100 indictments or arrests resulted from similar fraud in cities such as Detroit, Newark, Chicago, Cleveland, New Orleans, and Albany, New York. Too, there are occasional loners like the GS-3 clerk-typist who, after learning procedures in Internal Revenue's Office of International Operations in Washington, filed 14 returns seeking refunds totaling $21,000 for overseas Americans and had the checks mailed to post office boxes. (He was caught, not by IRS personnel's initiative, but because he cashed several checks in different names at one bank.) Perhaps the extent of the nation-wide problem of indiscretions is best reflected by IRS statistics of its disciplinary decisions:

	1964	1965
Total disciplinary actions	791	797
Reprimands, transfers, or demotions	467	422
Suspensions from job and pay	53	35
Employees separated from IRS*	271	340
Reasons:		
Bribery, extortion or collusion	40	62
Embezzlement or theft	15	15
Failure to pay proper tax	14	21
Falsification or distortion of IRS records	121	130
Unauthorized outside activity	9	10
Failure to discharge duties properly	2	11
Refusal to cooperate	3	2
Divulgence of confidential information	1	3
Acceptance of fees or gratuities	7	8
Personal and other misconduct	59	78

* Separations include resignations or retirement while employees were being investigated or before any disciplinary action was taken when derogatory information about an employee had been detected.

Basically the Internal Revenue Service uses two methods to prevent corruption among its employees. Most important, background investigations are made on all new IRS employees, regulations prohibit most outside activities (such as selling insurance) that would enable employees to legally shake down taxpayers, and possibilities of bribe offers are periodically emphasized. As Commissioner Sheldon Cohen has said: "We have made all of our employees aware at some time in their careers they might be approached. Whereas, the honest man's natural inclination is, if the subtle suggestion ever comes along, to say 'If you're trying to say what I think you are trying to say, forget it. I am not that kind of a fellow.' [But] if a man is inclined to try to corrupt some of our people, he may bounce around until he finds someone who has a particular weakness. He may be a good employee, but he may have financial difficulty at the moment and fall into this kind of trap."

Individuals won't "fall into a trap" if they are honest and, frequently, honest employees promptly report offers of bribes. Take, for example, the case that developed when Roger S. Davis, an agent in IRS's Boston District office, was investigating cabarets that possibly evaded the 10 percent excise tax added to a bill when entertainment occurs. When Davis noticed that Clauson's Inn in North Falmouth, Massachusetts, reported no excise tax but advertised in Boston's newspapers that it offered singing and dancing, he visited the Inn and heard the proprietor, German S. Lopez, deny that he placed the ad or had entertainment. That evening, Davis returned for a drink at Clauson's Inn, observed dancing, and then wrote a report that Lopez was a "potential delinquent" and that he would "follow up."

During the follow up, Davis, according to his version, told Lopez that he was liable for entertainment tax, was called into an office and asked if they could reach an "agreement" in order to avoid any "aggravation." After Davis replied that he couldn't drop the case, Lopez said that he didn't want to "insult" the agent. Then he laid some cash on the desk, remarking: "You can drop this case. Here's $200. Buy your wife a present. And I'll have more money for you at Christmas time. This is all I have now."

When Davis, who had not taken the money, estimated that Lopez's back taxes would total about $3,000 a year, Lopez laid another $220 on the desk and said that he didn't want to bother filing past returns but would file for the present quarter. He asked Davis, who picked up the $420, to return on October 24, three weeks later. On October 24—and after reporting the incident to his supervisor and told to "pretend to play along with the scheme" —Davis returned to Clauson's Inn with two miniature tape recorders in his pockets (one recorder failed to work) and a microphone disguised as a tie clasp. Inside Lopez's office, where Davis explained the IRS tax forms, this conversation was secretly recorded:

Lopez: Whatever we decided to do from here on I'd like you to be on my side and visit with me. Deduct anything you think you should and I'll be happy to . . . because you may prevent something coming up in the office. If you think I should be advised about it let me know. Pick up the phone. I can meet you in town or anywhere you want. . . .
Davis: Well, you know I've got a job to do.

Lopez: Yes and Uncle Sam is bigger than you and I are and we pay a lot of taxes, and if we can benefit something by it individually, let's keep it that way and believe me anything that transpires between you and I, not even my wife or accountant or anybody is aware of it. So I want you to feel that way about it.

Afterwards the pair discussed the Inn's three-year tax debt ($9,000) and, when Lopez called the figure "high," Davis interjected: "I don't want to get greedy or anything." Then Lopez handed the agent another $200, adding, "come in every so often and I'll give you a couple hundred dollars every time you come in." As Davis started to leave, Lopez remarked: "Now if you suggest that I should file returns from this point on, I'll do it. If you should suggest that I can get by without doing it, then just drop in every so often and I'll. . . ."

Although Lopez testified that he gave Davis the money to prepare his returns, he was convicted (and sentenced to one year in the penitentiary) on the basis of the tape recordings of trying to bribe the agent "to refrain . . . from computing a cabaret tax on . . . [the Inn's business] and from reporting same to the Internal Revenue Service."*

Not all of Internal Revenue's employees who are offered bribes, of course, voluntarily divulge the plot. Unquestionably, too, an even higher percentage of bribes would be accepted if it were not for Internal Revenue's second anticorruption measure: The Inspection Division. Supervised by Assistant Commissioner Vernon Acree, Inspection is divided into overlapping branches. Internal

* The Supreme Court upheld IRS's use of the recording as admissible evidence on grounds that "the government did not use an electronic device to listen in on conversations it could not otherwise have heard."

Audit is said to review Internal Revenue's "practices and procedures" and audit the personal tax returns and accompanying financial statements of IRS's management and supervisory personnel and most high-grade individuals in Audit, Intelligence, Collection, and Alcohol and Tobacco Tax Divisions. Internal Security investigates rumors and, particularly, possibilities of bribery, theft, extortion, collusion or indiscretions by IRS employees.

This work is done by 200 inspectors who are either former special agents or have equivalent background and training. These men work from regional offices and frequently rotate from region to region so that they aren't instantly recognized at IRS's district or regional offices. Once inside these offices, usually sections suspected of being corrupt, inspectors often operate like secret police, pretending to be a district or regional employee transferred to a new job against his wishes. Almost always, the inspectors are equipped with miniature tape recorders and microphones concealed in fake cigarette packages, ball-point pens and tie clasps, or hidden in offices and rest rooms and thereby enabling them to monitor even whispered conversations several rooms down the hall.

Inevitably, Inspection's presence or oft-rumored presence frightens some IRS employees much as IRS frightens taxpayers. Not infrequently, employees call Inspection "our CIA," "the police," "kangaroo cops" and "snoopers." And this fear—magnified by the fact that known inspectors often summon and interrogate certain employees —even moved some IRS employees in Newark, New Jersey, to hire the law firm of Royall, Koegal and Rogers to attempt to obtain a labor contract with Internal Revenue's management assuring what they called a reduction in "police state working conditions."

Yet, IRS employees who have nothing to hide theoretically have little to fear from Inspection—except possibly someone listening to an embarrassing conversation or snide criticism of IRS executives that otherwise might not have been heard. Too, periodic recording of conversation occasionally yields clues about employees' attitudes and rumors of potential bribery that seldom reach management level. Consider, for example, portions of a secretly recorded conversation at a party given at his apartment by one William Coady, an IRS undercover agent, between two employees in IRS's Audit Division in which a third Internal Revenue employee (who shall be called Walt) was mentioned and later tried on charges of accepting "illegal fees" from accountants:

Walt says to me, he says, "You know, Joe," he says, "you will never get in trouble," he says. "You are not greedy. I will never get rich either because I had some f—— accountant there carrying two f—— cases, you know, from friends of Frank, and everything, so you know he was supposed to be bringing me this and bringing me that and do this, you know. He bring shit. Closed it and said 'F—— him.' He said, "Did Walt ever see you?" he said. "What are you going to do?"

I said, "Listen, close them. F—— him, you know him, you know."

So he says he don't know, you know. Some time later he says to me, "You are not greedy, you will never get in trouble."

I said, "Listen, I can get into trouble no matter what."

"Well, you can get into trouble by getting—being greedy. Of course, you can get into trouble not being greedy, too. If you are dealing with a firm of partners, accountants, and one goes out right there, he says, "Well, f—— these guys, let them hang, okay, along with them he hangs you, too. That is why they got to know what goes on, too. They have got to know who, inspection and the director. They have got to know because I am sure like in all the time I have been there, there has been situations where some f—— thing has come up and you never heard about it. When I was up for the f—— interview, there, I told them there and the personnel, I said, listen, Bill, what is that thing? They asked me questions and I am wondering what have they got to do—and I wonder what they have got in that f—— folder, what have they got in my 201 file."*

Such opinions about Inspection, whether strongly biased (as in this case) or objective, are rarely heard by non-Internal Revenue employees. The image of Inspection that is advanced by IRS's public information and commissioner's offices is one of a supreme compliment: the "elite corps." In expressing these views, IRS personnel have even maintained that the 325 disclosures of internal frauds from 1961 to 1966 are no indication of an ensuing major scandal, but merely point up Inspection's proficiency in uncovering corruption.

While Inspection does seem reasonably proficient in proving corruption—and priority skills were required in detecting the aforementioned cases—it also must be noted that the investigations largely originated from taxpayers' rumors and, in some cases, divulged bribery that had transpired five years earlier. Moreover, Internal Revenue has demonstrated that Inspection can find what IRS's

---

* "Walt," the IRS employee named in the conversation, subsequently was convicted of accepting three bribes totaling $195, but the decision was reversed by the U.S. Court of Appeals: "We conclude that, in the circumstances of this case, the omission of criminal intent as one of the enumerated essential elements of the offense charged, constituted plain error and that, therefore, the judgment must be reversed and the case remanded for a new trial."

management wants it to find (or report) if such findings disagree with IRS's image.

An example of this practice occurred when the Senate Judiciary Subcommittee investigating invasions of privacy asked the Treasury Department—and then the IRS's commissioner—to clarify rumors that IRS agents illegally wiretapped telephones of taxpayers (not IRS employees). Such evidence would not appear difficult to locate. At least 128 agents had received instructions in wiretapping and many carried Kel-kits, which enabled them simply to insert a device into light sockets above public pay telephone booths and monitor conversations from automobiles. But after investigating six months, the commissioner's office first reported that Inspection had found no evidence of any wiretapping by IRS agents.

When the subcommittee's one investigator soon found at least six instances in which IRS agents tapped phones Commissioner Sheldon Cohen asked the subcommittee to allow the inspectors to continue the investigation. "We intend to get right to the bottom of this," Cohen testified at the subcommittee's hearings. "We feel it is right to be to the bottom of this fully and bring the committee the results of the investigation."

Responded Senator Edward Long: "I know that is your view, but doing it [the investigation] in the Department is like putting the fox in the hen house and locking up the henhouse for the night . . . This committee has uncovered this mess and called it to your attention."

IRS's apparent decision not to find any wiretapping by agents—and a responsible senator's incisive criticism—was a disturbing reminder of Internal Revenue's attitude 15 years earlier: "Don't interfere. Simply relay any allegations to us and we'll investigate, find the truth, and continue to insure integrity." Concealing wiretapping by IRS agents was a compromise, and any compromise within Internal Revenue can be extremely hazardous. The independent, noncompromising Inspection Division was created on July 19, 1951, as an aftermath of what was commonly called the "mess in Washington" and what was the bleakest scandal in Internal Revenue's history.

While none of Internal Revenue's present management was involved (nor is there any insinuation that equivalent practices exist) the episode is a historic lesson of what has occurred inside Internal Revenue without noncompromising vigilance. Until then, the Bureau of Internal Revenue was directed by a centralized commissioner through politically appointed District Collectors. Political they were. The situation was aptly summarized by a House Ways and Means Committee report:

In the selection of collectors, political considerations were often allowed to take precedence over needs of the office . . . In one state, the party organization forced replacement of a competent Collector of Internal Revenue by a new man, despite discovery by Bureau investigators that the new appointee was a tax evader . . . and this collector was shown to have resumed tax evasion while in office.

Consequently, internal corruption was so ingrained that only an outside investigator could expose it. That outsider appeared when John J. Williams, the co-owner of a cow feed store, surprisingly was elected a U.S. Senator from Delaware and soon was told by a constituent about a curious situation at Internal Revenue's office in Wilmington, Delaware: "Look, I paid my taxes and still got a bill and when I questioned it, was told to forget it. Same thing's happened to several people I know." Unfamiliar with investigative techniques, Williams solicited, and was advised, by Congress's General Accounting Office and Senator Styles Bridges, then chairman of the Senate Appropriations Committee, to have a former GAO investigator employed by the Committee obtain the list of tax delinquents in Internal Revenue's Wilmington office. When the investigator saw the list, however, he was embarrassed to deliver it to Williams. The notation, "Sen. J. J. Williams" appeared high among the delinquents. But Williams had paid his taxes. So had dozens of other "delinquent" taxpayers whom the Senator interviewed. After Williams disclosed his findings in the Senate, Internal Revenue found that a cashier in Wilmington had embezzled over 500 tax payments totaling $30,000 and, when he was about to be reported by a deputy collector, used Williams' check to help disguise his theft.

As taxpayers read about Williams' exposé, they literally deluged him with telephone calls and letters that almost had a recurrent theme: "If you think Delaware's bad, look in New York," etc. "But when I discussed the situation with several Internal Revenue officials," Williams recalls, "they seemed indifferent about straightening things out. Still I knew a crime had been committed and I'd be a part of it if I didn't expose it." Thus when Williams requested (but didn't receive) that office's list of taxpayers who owed more than $25,000, he walked into the Collectors Office of New York City's then Third District, introduced himself as "Mr. Williams," then pushed past a receptionist, into an executive's office, and walked out with the list. After gathering evidence, he rose in the Senate and denounced what he called a "disgraceful situation in New York."

Next Williams documented other situations which, he said, are "set up so the crooks get more in bribes than the government receives." He cited numerous cases such as the brewery in Indianapolis which had settled a $636,000 tax debt for $4,500 and then received a $35,000 *refund* from Internal Revenue. No reason for any suspicion except for one fact: The attorney in that case had been Joseph D. Nunan, Jr., former Commissioner of Internal Revenue who later served two years in prison for evading $91,086 in taxes on unreported income of $275,000. Furthermore, Williams added, certain high members of Internal Revenue were friends of organized criminals and had conspired to fix their income taxes. His evidence even included the license numbers of automobiles that allegedly were used as payoff sites. When an Internal Revenue employee hurriedly telephoned Williams that two "expert" agents had been "dogging" a certain hoodlum for two years, the Senator replied, "Get them here tomorrow morning." After the agents fumbled for answers to his questions, Williams realized that they knew little about the gangster's business. So he continued the crusade.

Afterwards, Williams revealed that 365-pound William G. ("Big Bill") Lias, then owner of Wheeling Downs Race Track, whom the FBI called a top mobster and ex-bootlegger, owed $2,230,744 in back income taxes and wouldn't pay even $500 taxes although he had $700,000 in a bank account. Told that Lias' case had been "settled," Williams opposed terms of the settlement: Lias would pay only 25 percent of his original tax debt and also escape penalties for 30 years of alleged fraud. Two days later, Internal Revenue filed liens against Lias and subsequently collected the full debt.

By this time Representative Cecil King had created a House Subcommittee to investigate Internal Revenue and found a virtual nationwide pattern to the corruption. Consider just one racket operated by Patrick Mooney while he was chief field deputy, office of Collector, in Internal Revenue's Nevada district. Mooney organized a paper corporation called Mountain City Consolidated Copper Company (MCCCC), a name that deceptively resembled a reputable firm, Mountain City Copper Company (MCCC). Although Mooney's MCCCC produced no copper ore and consisted of two log cabins, a tin toolshed, outdoor toilet and two air compressors sitting on a piece of land valued at approximately $12,000, the salesman easily sold 1,187,190 shares of MCCCC stock. The reason? Mooney, reported the Securities and Exchange Commission (SEC), "appears to be most persuasive in affecting stock sales. Many stockholders are owners of gambling clubs . . . who may be expected to court favor of employees of Internal Revenue." Then, after investigating complaints about MCCCC's worthless stock, the SEC elaborated with a specific charge: The tax returns of nine gambling casino owners had been under investigation for alleged tax fraud, but, after all nine bought enormous blocks of MCCCC stock, none was ever prosecuted. Two purchasers of stock admitted that MCCCC's salesman (who did not file tax returns for himself) had specifically told them their tax cases would be dropped if they bought stock.

Simultaneously, honest Internal Revenue agents even stumbled into evidence of Mooney's extortion. After Internal Revenue's San Francisco office filed liens for $800,000 in delinquent taxes and penalties against Elmer "Bones" Remmer, a reputed hoodlum, and then his gaudy Cal-Neva Lodge in Lake Tahoe, Nevada, special agents discovered in Remmer's records that a check payable to "Collector of Internal Revenue" for $7,724.11 had been voided. A check written for $5,324.11 and payable to Internal Revenue had been cashed. Then a check for the balance ($2,400) had been written to Mountain City Consolidated Copper Company, and cashed by Mooney, although no MCCCC stock had been issued to Remmer. Mooney, it turned out, had even prepared Remmer's tax return. But Mooney, then 80 years old and still collecting the nation's revenue, was exonerated by Internal Revenue officials. Finally, after the Congressional investigations ended, Mooney was convicted of tax fraud conspiracy.

Altogether Senator Williams and Representative King's subcommittee provided the impetus that resulted in 125 convictions of Internal Revenue personnel—including five high-ranking officials—for bribery, extortion and embezzlement, plus 681 dismissals or resignations.

Significantly, the scandal's exposure brought, not just the creation of the Inspection Division, but a desirable reorganization that placed Internal Revenue on the Civil Service's system of employee promotions based on merit, not political sponsorship, and eliminated all politically appointed positions except that of commissioner. Unquestionably, the improvement strengthened IRS's defense against internal fraud. For the next 10 years, Internal Revenue had no conspicuous corruption. Then, however, came the rumors and complaints in 1961 and Inspection's continual discovery thereafter of bribery or shakedowns by a minority of IRS employees who meet the public.

While only 1 percent of IRS's employees leave their jobs under dishonorable circumstances each year, the figure still is intolerable. As President Johnson said in his first meeting with IRS's leading officers in 1964, taxpayers "have every reason to expect from the men of the Internal Revenue Service total integrity, and integrity in tax administration is something we take for granted, but the price of integrity is eternal vigilance." This is why detecting internal corruption is just as important as detecting tax evaders.

Epilogue:
The Frightening Future

Ninety-nine percent of the Internal Revenue Service's effort—and 99 percent of all taxes it collects—goes to finance the pyramiding federal government. While the U.S. budget lists annual grants of $13.2 billion to state governments, this money is mostly earmarked for the 233 joint federal-state programs such as the War on Poverty and U.S. Interstate Highway construction program. Only about $1.2 billion of Internal Revenue's annual collections is allotted "without restriction of purpose" to underwrite governmental operations of our 50 states, 3,049 counties, 17,977 municipalities, 17,144 townships and 49,700 road, park and firefighting districts.

Yet these local jurisdictions, which have three times more employees (7,546,000) than the federal government, are responsible for the daily governmental functions that really affect the population. They conduct all elections, pass local laws, build and maintain public streets, parking spaces, parks, transportation systems, schools, colleges and universities, hospitals, mental health sanitariums, jails and water reservoirs, provide sanitation facilities, police and fire protection, welfare and unemployment payments, regulatory offices that range from building inspectors and zoning commissions to dog-catchers, and account for 25 percent of the nation's construction. Besides necessary expenditures to meet these demands, many state and local governments have such notorious patronage systems that there always appears to be two salaried pothole inspectors for every pothole.

Inevitably, state and local government expenses are increasing at a rate considered alarming even in comparison to federal expenditures. Between 1955 and 1965, state and local tax receipts increased 110 percent (while federal tax collections rose 70 percent) to $53.9 billion a year. Today, state and local taxes annually increase 9 percent—more than twice the national growth rate—and will exceed federal taxes by late 1970 and double every eight years thereafter. These taxes undoubtedly will increase even faster if the present trend continues. Thirty-two of 47 states with legislative sessions in 1965 enacted new taxes or raised existing taxes. And a 48th, Kentucky, whose legislature doesn't ordinarily meet during odd calendar years, was called into a special session to act on a measure increasing taxes.

Most large city governments are in such precarious financial straits that the mayor is preoccupied trying to raise taxes. In New York City, Boston and Detroit, for example, the financial situation is almost comparable to that of a semi-employed man who has a respectable reputation but spends twice as much money as he earns and can't get a loan. All three municipalities were given such low credit ratings (Baa—Lower Medium Grade) in 1965 by Moody's Investors Service that they must pay premium interest rates on loans to compensate lenders for the risk.

In prosperous 1966, when it borrowed $242 million to pay municipal expenses, New York City had to pay the highest interest since the Depression years.

Just how—considering that Internal Revenue already collects a burdensome income tax on most working adults —do states and cities raise taxes? By collecting taxes upon federally taxed income and levying hidden taxes. Among the methods:

36 states and 10 cities have an income tax.

37 states have a corporation tax.

40 states (encompassing 95 percent of the nation's population) have a general sales tax that ranges from 2 to 5 percent on expeditures for most merchandise or services.

50 states have a tax on gasoline that averages 7 cents a gallon.

48 states tax cigarettes (and tobacco) from 2 to 11 cents a package.

16 state governments operate all liquor stores within their boundaries and all 50 states tax liquor from $1.44 to $4 a gallon.

27 states received $355,206,308 in 1965 from parimutuel taxes on thoroughbred and harness racing.

40 cities levy a tax on hotel rooms.

50 states tax gifts, inheritances and even gross premiums paid to life insurance companies.

Virtually all localities have a property tax (on homes and real estate) and personal property tax (on automobiles, etc.). Then each state or city requires individuals to pay taxes to, progressively, build a home, and obtain a mortgage and deed for it. Motorists must annually buy a state license plate and city (or county) window decal to own an automobile, a tax to insure the vehicle, a license to drive it, and insert $125 million worth of coins in meters to park on a street—or face a fine, a doubly lucrative revenue source for most local governments.*

Additionally, many ctiizens pay local taxes—officially termed "fees" or "licenses"—to hunt, fish, marry, transfer stock, rent an office or safety deposit box, pay a utility bill, use a sewer, attend a sports event, sell cigarettes, whiskey, insurance, peanuts or candy, sail a boat or own a dog, pool table or bicycle. Perhaps the extent of local taxes (that usually overlap with federal levies) is best illustrated by two sets of facts: One, Tax Foundation, Inc., a private research organization, has counted 600 hidden taxes on a house, 151 taxes on a loaf of bread, 150 taxes on a lady's hat, and 116 taxes on a man's suit. Two, Louisiana has 47 different state taxes and 12 tax collection agencies, not including city and county taxes.

Wouldn't these taxation sources appear to be sufficient? Apparently they are not. Many states and localities have resorted to absurdities. For example, homeowners in Modesto, California, pay a "bedroom tax" of $15 for each new home and $5 for each bedroom. The measure was so inviting to politicians that the city council in nearby Newark, California, imposed a $50 annual tax on homeowners' first bedroom and $15 for each bedroom thereafter. Similar ingenuity occurred in another sunshine state, Florida. With a majority of Florida's legislators drinking from liquor bottles sitting on or near their desks and obviously intoxicated, they enacted a tax on drinking.

---

* North Dakota is the only state that has no parking meters—ever since one Howard Henry, a farmer, sued and won to have all meters removed on grounds that they were a nuisance that harmed business.

The tax was not on drinking liquor, but on consuming soft drinks at Florida's dog-racing tracks. In their more sober acts, the legislators increased taxes on citrus fruits and added a 5 percent tax on wholesale prices of bathing suits and accessories, plus diving, camping, hunting or fishing equipment.

New Hampshire, fumbling for ways to pay educational expenses, revived the discredited lottery, which it now bases upon a drawing and two horse races each fall. Predictably, soon after the first ticket was sold, at least 10 states had representatives study operations of the New Hampshire Sweepstakes with intentions of starting their own lotteries. Additionally, Detroit's City Council, which refused to legalize the sale of liquor on Sunday, allowed betting (and taxation) of dog racing on the Sabbath. Flagstaff, Arizona, simply imposed a blanket "business privilege" tax of 1 percent on all companies' gross receipts. Montana increased fees on sheep licenses and tried to push through a $5 service charge for processing state withholding tax returns.

If there is a refuge from burgeoning state and local taxes, the natural choice would appear to be remote Alaska. But Alaska not only has the nation's highest state income tax (3.2 to 14.6 percent) and liquor taxes ($4 per gallon), but it has a tax program that requires even artists, writers or handicrafters to pay $25 for an annual license. Still, Alaska's major cities cannot finance what would seem to be the most obvious need: plowing snow from the main streets. After the first big snowfall in 1965, for instance, Juneau had to impose a special realty tax to pay for large snow removals.

No tax burden, though, is as harsh as in New York City

and state. Residents must pay a 2 to 5 percent sales tax and a state income tax ranging from 2 to 10 percent of earnings, even on the amount of income paid to Internal Revenue for federal tax. Representative John Lindsay campaigned for election as mayor of New York on a program of ". . . new city taxes. None at all . . . I don't think that New York City can stand an income tax or a payroll tax." Then, callously, Mayor Lindsay demanded and received the City Council and State Legislature's approval of (1) a new city tax on incomes of businesses, residents and commuters and (2) a 25 percent increase in the tax on transferring stock—a move that had caused the New York Stock Exchange to threaten that it would relocate in New Jersey. Next Lindsay termed "deeply regrettable" the City Council Committee on Finance's second postponement of a prior request to increase annual real estate taxes from 2¼ to 3 percent of the assessed value. Then the City tax department readjusted what it called the real estate tax's "basic rate" by 40 cents per $100, subtly increasing annual taxes on a house valued at $10,000 from $456 to $496. Already New York City collected the customary local gimmick taxes, plus fees for planting a tree on one's own property and disposing of a dead pet. And the municipal tax collectors had (until late 1966) authority to add arbitrarily 12 percent to any taxpayer's bill if he or she merely questioned or disagreed with the collector's assessment!

Even extra pennies are literally squeezed from New York's existing sources of taxes without apparent regard for the consequences. Take, as one example, horse racing. New York's State Tax Bureau collects nearly $140 million a year from racing in pari-mutuel taxes and "breakage," the pennies left over when payoffs are figured to the nearest nickel. While the $140 million is eight times more money than Nevada receives in taxes from legalized gaming casinos, New York politicians wanted more. The State compelled racetracks to make payoffs only to the nearest dime and give it most of the pennies. The move brought New York $7,742,453 in breakage in 1965, caused racing attendance to decline, and the Thoroughbred Owners and Breeder's Association to warn it could destroy horse racing. And to accelerate the flow of pennies and pari-mutuel taxes into the State Tax Bureau, New York extended the horse-racing season from January 3 to December 15 despite the fact that the tracks' racing surfaces often are dangerously frozen during the beginning and end of the racing season.

Take, as a second example, cigarettes. Already a package of cigarettes was directly taxed 8 cents by the U.S. government, 4 cents by New York City, and 5 cents by New York state. In 1965, New York piously raised its state cigarette tax to 10 cents, thus increasing the total tax on a package of cigarettes to 22 cents, or more than half of the total price of 43 cents. Then, naively, politicians sat back and calculated how many additional millions of dollars in cigarette taxes would arrive by mail. However, the extra taxes didn't arrive, legal retail cigarette sales fell 26 percent in New York, and the Wholesale Tobacco Distributors of New York, Inc., revealed in a private report:

The tremendous drop in cigarette sales suffered by legitimate business people has placed them in such desperate financial straits that many retail stores are closing, jobbers are going out of business, and venders, unable to meet machine payments and other financial obligations, have either sold their businesses or given up.

Whereupon politicians nearly panicked: "Organized bootleggers . . . the Mafia . . . the Cosa Nostra . . . smugglers," the politicians roared. They were buying cigarettes for $1.83 to $2 a carton (New York retail price: $4.20 a carton) in North Carolina, one of two states with no local cigarette taxes, and smuggling them up Tobacco Road—U.S. Highway 301 out of North Carolina—and re-selling them in New York. The state and city were being "robbed" of $40 million a year in taxes. Tax collectors warned of $250 fines and a year in jail for "illegal importa-tion." Roadblocks were said to be on all main arteries. The Coast Guard was said to have been summoned. Empha-sized Joseph H. Murphy, commissioner of the New York State Tax Bureau: "We have 16 men [and later 60] tackling the job, working 16-hour shifts at the bridge and tunnel entrances to New York City."

True, there was some organized smuggling. After one four-day stake-out—with pistols and cameras—two under-cover detectives managed to contact two men from Alexandria, Virginia, who said they were in the "buying and selling business" but who would never qualify for Mafia membership. The pair arranged for the detectives to meet a third man driving a U-haul truck filled with cigarettes said to have been purchased for $3,200 in Washington, D.C. (where taxes are only 2 cents a pack-age). Still, if politicians stood during the morning rush at the entrances to the Lincoln and Hudson Tunnels leading into Manhattan, they would see cartons of cigarettes stacked on front seats of automobiles with neighboring

New Jersey and Connecticut license plates. Many residents of New York simply have commuting acquaintances buy their cigarettes in New Jersey or Connecticut—where cigarette taxes are 11 to 14 cents less per package.

The origin of the state tax crisis dates back to 1913. When the states ratified the Constitution's 16th Amendment that gave the federal government a carte blanche to tax personal incomes, they voted away their principle source of revenue. Since then, the legislators who sit under the state capitol domes and originate tax laws have steadily magnified their problem. Today, many of the nation's 7,708 state legislators and 99 legislative houses, aside from occasionally being bound by archaic state constitutions on taxation, are a carnival of triviality, inefficiency, opportunism, conflict of interest, and blatant corruption. Even the sales tax itself reflects some of the comical reasoning. Indiana's legislators, for example, decided that ice used in cocktails or alcoholic beverages would not be subject to sales tax but ice used to cool bottled soft drinks or watermelons would be taxed. New York's legislators determined that there would be no sales tax on popcorn if it was salted and buttered, such as the type sold in movie houses; but there would be a sales tax on popcorn if it was covered with caramel, such as Cracker Jack. The same men voted not to tax tuna fish sold for human consumption, but to tax tuna that was packaged for cats.

Other problems stem from a harsh cycle. States must obtain new industry in order to provide jobs (and collect taxes) for its residents. Yet about the only way a poorer state can attract, say, a new General Electric plant is to exempt the corporation from most state or local taxes for 10 to 12 years.

Finally the cities and counties, who have been left what often is called the "taxation crumbs," have multiple difficulties collecting the crumbs. For one thing, about half of the cities have not yet been given home rule by state legislations. Thus even the nation's two largest cities, New York and Chicago, must appeal to the comparatively minute capitals of Albany, New York, and Springfield, Illinois, respectively, for permission to increase the price of dog tags or revise any tax law. For another, localities raise about 90 percent of their revenue by taxing property and, suddenly, that source is evaporating. Why? A majority of the middle- and upper-income families are moving from highly taxed property in large cities to suburbs, then commuting to the city to work. Large cities are being filled with Negroes and low-income families, who usually settle in government-subsidized, tax-exempt housing or create a perimeter of new, lightly taxed slums faster than old slums can be eradicated. What old slums (previously yielding *some* taxes) have been cleared by urban renewal programs are replaced by nontaxed public buildings, parking lots and playgrounds.

Consequently, appraised values—and property taxes— have become so high in some choice residential neighborhoods that tax-exempt foundations, social and veterans' clubs, religious, scientific and labor organizations, and governments have begun to dominate the areas. Since these organizations have the advantage over private citizens of paying little or no taxes, they have ventured into such extensive real estate speculation that an estimated 32 percent of all property in cities is now officially untaxable.

Similarly tax-exempt groups have entered the big business category. Examples: New York's famous Yankee Stadium is owned by the Catholic Knights of Columbus and leased back to private interests. New Orleans' commercial radio station, WWL, is owned by the Jesuit Loyola University. And the Biltmore Hotel in Dayton, Ohio, is owned by the First Baptist, First Christian and Second Presbyterian Churches of Bloomington, Illinois. Warns Paul Corusy, executive director of the International Association of Assessing Officers: "The property tax base is being so seriously eroded that an equitable distribution of the property tax load is more myth than fact."

This widespread tax exemption also means that about $75 of every $375 that property owners are assessed in taxes is caused by a privileged organization's tax immunity. Such increasing taxes in many well-kept middle-class neighborhoods cause particular hardships to individuals on fixed incomes or pensions. In an extreme case in New York's Astoria, Queens, during 1966, a Mrs. Mary Callaghan Purcell—she was 103 years old at the time—told the Kew Gardens branch of the New York City collector's office: "I've paid taxes long enough and I'm not paying anymore." Since Mrs. Purcell owed approximately $2,500 in taxes over a four-year period, the city seized and auctioned the home for $20,000 (and invoked a law that allows it to keep the entire $20,000, not just the $2,500 that was due for taxes).

What, besides enacting new or increasing old taxes, is being done to alleviate the nonfederal governments' dilemma? In essence, state tax bureaus are voluntarily being transformed into virtual extensions of the Internal Revenue Service. Under a Federal-State Cooperative Program,

Internal Revenue is training state tax administrators and has agreements with 40 states and the District of Columbia to exchange information on individual and corporate tax returns. Accordingly, IRS furnishes the states duplicate lists of individuals and businesses who have not filed returns, have been audited and assessed additional taxes, or (after the case is settled) are involved in an alleged tax fraud. This information enables the states to levy about $25 million a year in additional taxes—or from 11 to 85 percent of each state's total deficiency collections. (Internal Revenue also receives about $7 million a year in taxes by developing information from states.) And in the first step to assist local taxing authorities, Internal Revenue began in 1966 (upon Governor William Scranton's request) to supply Pennsylvania's 67 counties with names of taxpayers whose returns list ownership of stocks, bonds and other property in order to improve the counties' honor system of collecting taxes on personal property.

While states have increasingly benefited from IRS's concurrence, the additional receipts will not offset mounting debts in any but a few states. Perhaps the states' only practical answer—apart from economizing—is a share-the-taxes plan originated by Walter Heller, former chairman of the President's Council of Economic Advisers, seconded by most governors, and, on April 6, 1966, formally recommended by the Republican Coordinating Committee. The Committee's proposal:

(1) Return to the States a gradually increasing portion of the personal and corporate income taxes collected by the Federal Government, starting with two percent of the collection the first year the plan was in effect and increasing to 10 percent in eight years.

(2) Institute a system of Federal grants to the States in broad, functional areas such as mental health, education, water pollution control, highway and the like, "with a minimum of supervisory controls" and without trying to dictate the precise nature of the programs, thereby enabling the States to spend the money in their own way on needs they find most pressing.

The proposal, which would not allow states to repeal their existing taxes, certainly would slow the sweeping increases in taxes. But even if the unlikely occurred and the plan was adopted, any substantial amount of federal taxes returned to the states would be recovered by raising the sum that individuals and businesses now pay to the Internal Revenue Service. Whatever happens, American taxpayers have only one foreseeable future: a frightening future.

Index

239